The Pampered Chef®
ALL THE BEST
FROM OUR KITCHENS TO YOURS

When your family is gathered around the dinner table, you want to be sure you are serving them the very best. In The Pampered Chef Test Kitchens, we believe that certain tried-and-true recipes in our repertoire serve as the inspiration and unwavering standard for each new recipe we create. These spectacular recipes are in constant demand from our customers and are overwhelmingly popular because they are quick, easy and delicious. It seemed only natural that we gather them together in *All The Best*, a collection of time-honored favorites we are sure you will use again and again.

Not only will you find these must-have recipes to be an essential addition to your own kitchen, but you will also discover some foolproof variations that you'll embrace just like the original. And, as a special feature of the cookbook, we have developed a system of mix-and-match fillings for our most celebrated recipe creations, the Braid, Ring and Wreath, along with step-by-step photography to ensure you have the same success that we have.

As always, all of these classics and up-and-coming recipe favorites have been developed, tasted and tested in our very own Test Kitchens. Each recipe is beautifully photographed in full color and is supported by Cook's Tips to help guide you through shopping and food preparation. As a result, you will put a wonderful meal on the table and be able to spend more time with your family.

With timeless recipes, tips and kitchen tools from The Pampered Chef, we know you will turn to *All The Best* to inspire magnificent meals for you and your loved ones. From our kitchens to yours, we wish you all the best.

Enjoy!

The Pampered Chef Test Kitchens

On the cover: Cool & Creamy Chocolate Fondue (p. 96)

CONTENTS

Just for STARTERS 4

A collection of bites to get meals started right.

Here you'll find some of our most celebrated appetizers, snacks and bite-size treats whether it's for a last-minute teen gathering, a neighborhood potluck party or a special celebration. For a fabulous, no-fuss start to any get-together, *Tomato-Basil Squares* wins rave reviews. Looking for something light, easy and elegant? *Lemon Pepper Crab Canapés* will easily please busy hosts and guests alike. When you want simple, tasty nibblers that can be assembled just in time for halftime, *Game Day Party Mix* or *Hot Pizza Dip* score big. So jump-start your next gathering with a selection of our most-asked-for appetizers and get ready to share in the fun!

Clubhouse Chicken Squares (p. 9)

Beef Taco Ring (p. 80)

Let's Get TOGETHER..........46

Dinner, lunch... and even brunch.

We think you'll be delighted to add these outstanding recipes to your collection of family favorites. These tried-and-true recipes, along with many great new variations, are quick, easy and sure to win over the most finicky family members. Whether serving brunch, lunch or dinner, we offer plenty of ideas to inspire the busy cooks in your family. For a fresh and fabulous start to the weekend, *Florentine Brunch Casserole* is a true eye-opener. For a satisfying lunch, *Savory Sandwich Ring* fits the bill with a variety of deli sandwich selections to choose from. When the family wants a break from the ordinary, pair *Fabulous Fajita Pizza* with *Fresh Salsa & Guacamole Duo* from our appetizer chapter and you've created a mealtime sensation they'll never tire of. And, with our popular braid, ring and wreath recipes, the hardest part of meal planning will be choosing from among our menu of fabulous fillings. Dinner is a sure winner when you turn to these pages for inspiration.

Save Room for
DESSERT

From simple treats to dazzling sweets.

No one will pass up dessert when the menu includes a signature sweet treat from The Pampered Chef®. From simple cookies to luscious cakes, these time-honored classics will lift everyone's spirits after a hard day's work. Who could resist light and refreshing *Heavenly Lemon Angel Cake* after a summer meal on the patio? *Taffy Apple Pizza* and *Easy Peanut Butter Presses* are perfect back-to-school treats for your little troupers. For something warm, rich and ultra-tempting, turn to *Turtle Fudge Skillet Cake* and sweep drop-in guests off their feet. Always in season, these delectable dessert recipes will finish off any meal in style.

Cherry Almond Angel Roll (p. 86)

Just for STARTERS

A collection
of bites
to get meals
started right.

*Hot Pizza Dip (p. 7), Toasted Baguette Slices
(p. 7), Mini Ham Puffs (p. 6)*

- It is helpful to use a ruler as a guide while you cut the dough into squares.

- Dijon mustard originally comes from Dijon, France. It is made from brown mustard seeds, white wine, unfermented grape juice and a blend of seasonings.

MINI HAM PUFFS

Prep time: 20 minutes • Bake time: 12-14 minutes

Guests will love these savory gems. Serve them hot from the oven with additional Dijon mustard. (Pictured on p. 4-5)

1	package (2.5 ounces) processed ham or smoked turkey, finely chopped
2	tablespoons finely chopped onion
1/2	cup (2 ounces) shredded Swiss or cheddar cheese
1	egg
1	tablespoon snipped fresh parsley
1 1/2	teaspoons Dijon mustard
1/8	teaspoon ground black pepper
1	package (8 ounces) refrigerated crescent rolls

1. Preheat oven to 350°F. Lightly spray **Deluxe Mini-Muffin Pan** with vegetable oil using **Kitchen Spritzer**. Finely chop ham and onion using **Food Chopper**; place in **Small Batter Bowl**. Add cheese, egg, parsley, mustard and black pepper; mix well.

2. Unroll crescent dough and press into one large rectangle. Cut dough into 24 squares using **Pizza Cutter**. Press one square of dough into each muffin cup using lightly floured **Mini-Tart Shaper**.

3. Using **Small Scoop**, fill each muffin cup with a scant scoop of ham mixture. Bake 12-14 minutes or until puffs are light golden brown. Remove from pan; serve immediately.

Yield: 24 appetizers

Nutrients per serving (2 appetizers): Calories 110, Total Fat 6 g, Saturated Fat 2 g, Cholesterol 25 mg, Carbohydrate 8 g, Protein 4 g, Sodium 260 mg, Fiber 0 g

Diabetic exchanges per serving (2 appetizers): 1/2 starch, 1/2 meat, 1/2 fat (1/2 carb)

HOT PIZZA DIP

Prep time: 15 minutes • Bake time: 15-20 minutes

Who can resist this bubbly, pizza-flavored dip? Serve it in the Mini-Baker to keep it warm until the last bite. (Pictured on p. 4-5)

1 package (8 ounces) cream cheese, softened

1 teaspoon **Pantry Italian Seasoning Mix**

1 cup (4 ounces) shredded mozzarella cheese

¾ cup (3 ounces) grated fresh Parmesan cheese

1 can (8 ounces) pizza sauce

¼ cup diced green bell pepper, sliced green onions or chopped pitted ripe olives

Toasted Baguette Slices (recipe follows)

1. Preheat oven to 350°F. In **Small Batter Bowl**, combine cream cheese and seasoning mix; spread onto bottom of **Mini-Baker**.

2. In small bowl, combine mozzarella and Parmesan cheeses. Sprinkle half of the mozzarella cheese mixture over cream cheese mixture. Top with pizza sauce, spreading evenly. Sprinkle with remaining mozzarella cheese mixture. Bake 15-20 minutes or until bubbly. Top with bell pepper. Serve with *Toasted Baguette Slices*.

Yield: 2½ cups (20 servings)

Nutrients per serving (2 tablespoons dip): Calories 80, Total Fat 6 g, Saturated Fat 4 g, Cholesterol 20 mg, Carbohydrate 2 g, Protein 4 g, Sodium 200 mg, Fiber 0 g

Diabetic exchanges per serving (2 tablespoons dip): ½ meat, 1 fat (0 carb)

- To heat *Hot Pizza Dip* in the microwave oven, microwave on HIGH 2 minutes; turn. Microwave on HIGH 2-3 minutes or until mixture is bubbly and heated through.

- Italian seasoning can be substituted for the Italian Seasoning Mix, if desired.

TOASTED BAGUETTE SLICES

Prep time: 5 minutes • Bake time: 10-12 minutes

These crispy bread slices can be served with dips, salads or soups. (Pictured on p. 4-5)

24 slices French bread, cut ¼ inch thick

2 tablespoons olive oil

1. Preheat oven to 375°F. Place bread slices on **Rectangle Stone**; lightly brush tops with olive oil. Bake 10-12 minutes or until lightly browned.

Yield: 24 slices

Nutrients per serving (2 slices): Calories 190, Total Fat 4 g, Saturated Fat .5 g, Cholesterol 0 mg, Carbohydrate 33 g, Protein 6 g, Sodium 380 mg, Fiber 2 g

Diabetic exchanges per serving (2 slices): 2 starch, ½ fat (2 carb)

CLUBHOUSE CHICKEN SQUARES

Prep time: 25 minutes • Bake time: 12-15 minutes
Cool time: 45 minutes • Chill time: 30 minutes

Smoky bacon, crispy cucumber and shredded cheddar cheese highlight these tasty appetizer squares.

2 packages (8 ounces each) refrigerated crescent rolls

1 package (8 ounces) cream cheese, softened

2 tablespoons mayonnaise

1 small garlic clove, pressed

1 teaspoon **Pantry All-Purpose Dill Mix** (optional)

1 can (10 ounces) chunk white chicken, drained and flaked

½ small cucumber, seeded, sliced and quartered

2 plum tomatoes, seeded and diced

½ cup (2 ounces) shredded cheddar cheese

6 slices bacon, crisply cooked, drained and crumbled

1. Preheat oven to 375°F. Unroll one package of crescent rolls across one end of **Stoneware Bar Pan** with longest sides of dough across width of pan. Repeat with remaining package of dough, filling pan. Using **Baker's Roller™**, roll dough to seal perforations and press up sides to form crust. Bake 12-15 minutes or until golden brown. Remove from oven; cool completely.

2. In **Classic Batter Bowl**, combine cream cheese, mayonnaise, garlic pressed with **Garlic Press** and dill mix, if desired; mix well. Spread cream cheese mixture evenly over crust; top with chicken.

3. Thinly slice cucumber using **Ultimate Slice & Grate** fitted with adjustable thin slicing blade; cut slices into quarters. Dice tomatoes using **Chef's Knife**. Grate cheese using **Deluxe Cheese Grater**. Sprinkle cucumber, tomatoes, cheese and bacon over chicken. Refrigerate 30 minutes. Cut into squares.

Yield: 12 servings

Nutrients per serving (2 squares): Calories 300, Total Fat 20 g, Saturated Fat 8 g, Cholesterol 45 mg, Carbohydrate 17 g, Protein 11 g, Sodium 560 mg, Fiber less than 1 g

Diabetic exchanges per serving (2 squares): 1 starch, 1 meat, 3 fat (1 carb)

COOK'S TIPS

- Reduced-fat crescent rolls, reduced-fat cream cheese (Neufchâtel) and reduced-fat mayonnaise can be substituted for the crescent rolls, cream cheese and mayonnaise, if desired.

- Dried dill weed can be substituted for the All-Purpose Dill Mix, if desired.

- If desired, 1½ cups chopped cooked chicken can be substituted for the canned chicken.

- Use **The Corer™** to easily remove the seeds from the cucumber before slicing.

- Our **Cook's Corer™** is a handy tool for effortlessly removing the stems from tomatoes and strawberries.

Unfold second crust and place over crust on baking stone, matching edges.

Using **Baker's Roller**™, roll both crusts out together to edge of baking stone.

Using smooth end of pastry tool, form a decorative fluted edge.

GREEK ISLANDS PASTRY

Prep time: 25 minutes • Bake time: 20-25 minutes • Cool time: 10 minutes

A flaky pastry crust is spread with a creamy spinach and feta cheese filling, then topped with a delicious artichoke mixture. Taste a slice of Greece!

Crust

- 1 package (15 ounces) refrigerated pie crusts (2 crusts)
- ¼ cup (1 ounce) grated fresh Parmesan cheese, divided

Filling

- 1 package (10 ounces) frozen chopped spinach, thawed and well drained
- 1 package (8 ounces) cream cheese, softened
- 1 package (4 ounces) crumbled feta cheese
- 1 garlic clove, pressed

Toppings

- 1 can (14 ounces) artichoke hearts in water, drained and chopped
- 1 lemon
- 1 can (3.5 ounces) pitted ripe olives, drained and sliced
- 1½ teaspoons **Pantry Italian Seasoning Mix**
- 3 plum tomatoes, sliced

1. Preheat oven to 375°F. Let pie crusts stand at room temperature 15 minutes. Lightly sprinkle **Large Round Stone** with flour. Unfold one pie crust and place in center of baking stone. Lightly brush with water using **Pastry Brush**. Using **Deluxe Cheese Grater**, grate half of the Parmesan cheese over crust.

2. Unfold second crust and place over crust on baking stone, matching edges and pressing down to seal. Roll both crusts out together to edge of baking stone. Fold ½ inch of edge of crust in toward center, forming an even border; press to seal seam. Flute edge of crust as desired. Prick bottom of crust using pastry tool. Bake 20-25 minutes or until golden brown. Remove from oven; cool 10 minutes.

3. For filling, in **Classic Batter Bowl**, combine spinach, cream cheese, feta cheese and garlic pressed with **Garlic Press**; mix well. Spread spinach mixture evenly over crust.

4. For toppings, chop artichokes using **Food Chopper**. Zest lemon using **Lemon Zester/Scorer**. In **Small Batter Bowl**, combine artichokes, lemon zest, olives and seasoning mix; mix well. Spoon artichoke topping evenly over filling; top with tomato slices. Grate remaining Parmesan cheese over tomatoes. Cut into wedges.

Yield: 12 servings

Nutrients per serving: Calories 280, Total Fat 19 g, Saturated Fat 9 g, Cholesterol 35 mg, Carbohydrate 23 g, Protein 7 g, Sodium 420 mg, Fiber 3 g

Diabetic exchanges per serving: 1 starch, 1 vegetable, 4 fat (1 carb)

SAVORY VEGETABLE MINI QUICHES

Prep time: 30 minutes • Bake time: 17-20 minutes

Serve these bite-size tarts in style on our Simple Additions™ Rectangle Platter.

1 package (15 ounces) refrigerated pie crusts (2 crusts)
½ cup milk
2 eggs
4 slices bacon, crisply cooked, drained and chopped
½ cup finely chopped zucchini
½ cup finely chopped mushrooms
1 green onion with top, sliced
½ cup (2 ounces) shredded cheddar cheese
1 garlic clove, pressed
   Dash of ground black pepper

1. Preheat oven to 375°F. Let pie crusts stand at room temperature 15 minutes. Lightly spray **Deluxe Mini-Muffin Pan** with vegetable oil using **Kitchen Spritzer**. Whisk milk and eggs in **Classic Batter Bowl**.

2. Chop bacon, zucchini and mushrooms using **Food Chopper**. Add bacon, zucchini, mushrooms, green onion, cheese, garlic pressed with **Garlic Press** and black pepper to batter bowl; set aside.

3. On lightly floured surface, roll one crust to a 12-inch circle using **Baker's Roller**.™ Using **Scalloped Bread Tube**, cut out 12 pastry pieces. Press one pastry piece into each muffin cup using **Mini-Tart Shaper**. Repeat with remaining crust to fill remaining muffin cups.

4. Using **Small Scoop**, fill each muffin cup with a rounded scoop of vegetable mixture. Bake 17-20 minutes or until crusts are light golden brown. Cool in pan 2 minutes; carefully remove mini quiches from pan. Serve warm.

Yield: 24 appetizers

Nutrients per serving (1 mini quiche): Calories 100, Total Fat 6 g, Saturated Fat 3 g, Cholesterol 25 mg, Carbohydrate 9 g, Protein 2 g, Sodium 110 mg, Fiber 0 g

Diabetic exchanges per serving (1 mini quiche): ½ starch, 1 fat (½ carb)

TOMATO-BASIL SQUARES

Prep time: 30 minutes • Bake time: 15-20 minutes

Boasting the garden-fresh flavors of ripe tomatoes, basil and two kinds of cheese, this quick and easy appetizer is unforgettable.

1 package (10 ounces) refrigerated pizza crust
2 cups (8 ounces) shredded mozzarella cheese, divided
¼ cup (1 ounce) grated fresh Parmesan cheese
⅔ cup mayonnaise
2 tablespoons snipped fresh basil leaves
1 garlic clove, pressed
4 plum tomatoes, sliced

1. Preheat oven to 375°F. Using lightly floured **Baker's Roller™**, roll pizza crust to within 1 inch of edge of **Rectangle Stone**. Sprinkle crust with 1 cup of the mozzarella cheese; set aside.

2. Using **Deluxe Cheese Grater**, grate Parmesan cheese into **Small Batter Bowl**. Add remaining mozzarella cheese, mayonnaise, basil and garlic pressed with **Garlic Press**; mix well.

3. Using **Ultimate Slice & Grate** fitted with v-shaped blade, slice tomatoes; arrange evenly over crust. Using **Medium Scoop**, scoop cheese mixture evenly over tomatoes; spread evenly. Bake 15-20 minutes or until crust is golden brown. Cut into squares; serve warm.

Yield: 20 servings

Nutrients per serving (1 square): Calories 130, Total Fat 9 g, Saturated Fat 2.5 g, Cholesterol 15 mg, Carbohydrate 8 g, Protein 4 g, Sodium 210 mg, Fiber 0 g

Diabetic exchanges per serving (1 square): ½ starch, ½ meat, 1 fat (½ carb)

HAWAIIAN DIP WITH FRUIT KEBABS

Prep time: 30 minutes • Chill time: 30 minutes

The islands inspired this refreshing dip made with juicy pineapple and sweet coconut.

- To toast coconut, preheat oven to 350°F. Spread coconut onto **Small Bar Pan**. Bake 10-12 minutes or until light golden brown; cool completely.

- Cut apples into wedges using the **Apple Wedger** then cut into chunks with the **Paring Knife**.

- Cut bananas into chunks using the **Crinkle Cutter**, if desired.

- Scoop cantaloupe and honeydew into balls using the **Small Scoop**.

- Dip the apple and banana chunks into lemon juice to prevent browning. Use the **Juicer** to get the most juice from fresh lemons.

Dip

- ¾ cup milk
- ½ cup sour cream
- 1 package (3.4 ounces) vanilla instant pudding and pie filling
- 1 can (8 ounces) crushed pineapple in juice, undrained
- ½ cup sweetened flaked coconut, toasted, divided
- 1 lime

Kebabs

- 6-8 cups assorted fruits such as apples, bananas and pineapple, cut into 1-inch chunks, cantaloupe and honeydew melon balls and whole strawberries and grapes

1. For dip, combine milk, sour cream and pudding mix in **Small Batter Bowl**; whisk until smooth.

2. Stir in pineapple with juice and ⅓ cup of the coconut. Zest lime using **Lemon Zester/Scorer** to measure 1 teaspoon zest. Juice lime to measure 1 teaspoon juice. Stir lime zest and juice into dip. Cover and refrigerate at least 30 minutes before serving.

3. For kebabs, alternately thread fruit onto twenty-four 6-inch wooden skewers. Spoon dip into serving bowl; sprinkle with remaining coconut. Serve with kebabs.

Yield: 12 servings

Nutrients per serving (3 tablespoons dip, 2 kebabs): Calories 130, Total Fat 4 g, Saturated Fat 3 g, Cholesterol 10 mg, Carbohydrate 24 g, Protein 2 g, Sodium 140 mg, Fiber 2 g

Diabetic exchanges per serving (3 tablespoons dip, 2 kebabs): 1½ starch, ½ fat (1½ carb)

Hawaiian Dip with Fruit Kebabs, Apple Berry Salsa (p. 18), Baked Cinnamon Chips (p. 19)

- The Apple Peeler/ Corer/Slicer works best with fresh, firm, uniformly shaped apples and potatoes.

- Mashed potatoes are done in a flash when you slice the potatoes using the Apple Peeler/ Corer/Slicer before cooking them. For a more rustic and nutritional dish, scrub potatoes thoroughly before slicing them, leaving the peels on.

APPLE BERRY SALSA

Prep time: 15 minutes

Serve this popular fruit salsa with Baked Cinnamon Chips for a unique appetizer or refreshingly light dessert. (Pictured on p. 17)

2 medium Granny Smith apples
1 pint strawberries, diced (about 1½ cups)
2 kiwi, peeled and diced
1 small orange
2 tablespoons packed brown sugar
2 tablespoons apple jelly or apricot jam
Baked Cinnamon Chips (p. 19)

1. Peel, core and slice apples using **Apple Peeler/Corer/Slicer**. Coarsely chop apple slices using **Food Chopper**. Dice strawberries and kiwi using **Chef's Knife**. Place fruit in **Small Batter Bowl**.

2. Zest orange using **Lemon Zester/Scorer** to measure 1 teaspoon zest. Juice orange using **Juicer** to measure 2 tablespoons juice. Add orange zest, juice, brown sugar and jelly to fruit mixture; mix gently. Refrigerate until ready to serve.

3. Spoon into serving bowl. Serve with *Baked Cinnamon Chips*.

Yield: 3 cups (16 servings)

Low Fat Nutrients per serving (3 tablespoons salsa): Calories 30, Total Fat 0 g, Saturated Fat 0 g, Cholesterol 0 mg, Carbohydrate 8 g, Protein 0 g, Sodium 0 mg, Fiber 1 g

Diabetic exchanges per serving (3 tablespoons salsa): ½ fruit (½ carb)

BAKED TORTILLA CHIPS

Prep time: 5 minutes • Bake time: 8-10 minutes per batch

These chips are light, crispy and so easy to make! (Pictured on p. 24)

8 (7-inch) flour tortillas

1. Preheat oven to 400°F. Cut each tortilla into eight wedges; arrange half of the tortilla wedges in a single layer on **Large Round Stone**. Bake 8-10 minutes or until edges are lightly browned and crisp.

2. Remove from baking stone; cool completely. Repeat with remaining tortilla wedges.

Yield: 64 chips (16 servings)

Low Fat Nutrients per serving (4 chips): Calories 40, Total Fat 1 g, Saturated Fat 0 g, Cholesterol 0 mg, Carbohydrate 6 g, Protein 1 g, Sodium 130 mg, Fiber less than 1 g

Diabetic exchanges per serving (4 chips): ½ starch (½ carb)

Variations: *Baked Cinnamon Chips*
(Pictured on p. 17): Lightly spray tortillas with water. Combine 1 tablespoon sugar and ¼ teaspoon ground cinnamon in **Flour/Sugar Shaker**. Sprinkle cinnamon sugar evenly over tortillas. Cut each tortilla into eight wedges and bake as directed above. Cool completely.

Chocolate-Drizzled Cinnamon Chips
(Pictured on p. 97): Prepare *Baked Cinnamon Chips* as recipe directs. Place ½ cup semi-sweet chocolate morsels in **Small Micro-Cooker®**; microwave, uncovered, on HIGH 1-1½ minutes, stirring after each 20-second interval or until chocolate is melted and smooth. Drizzle chocolate evenly over cinnamon chips; let stand until set.

HOT ARTICHOKE & SPINACH DIP

Prep time: 15 minutes • Bake time: 20-25 minutes

This updated classic uses creamed spinach to create the tastiest, creamiest hot dip ever!

1   jar (6 ounces) marinated artichoke hearts, drained and coarsely chopped
1   package (9-11 ounces) frozen creamed spinach, thawed
¼   cup mayonnaise
¼   cup sour cream
1   small garlic clove, pressed
½   cup (2 ounces) grated fresh Parmesan cheese
    Diced red bell pepper (optional)
    Baked Pita Chips (recipe follows)

1. Preheat oven to 375°F. Coarsely chop artichokes using **Food Chopper**; place in **Small Batter Bowl**. Add spinach, mayonnaise and sour cream.

2. Press garlic into batter bowl using **Garlic Press**. Grate Parmesan cheese into batter bowl using **Deluxe Cheese Grater**; mix well. Spoon into **Small Oval Baker**.

3. Bake 20-25 minutes or until heated through. Garnish with bell pepper, if desired. Serve with *Baked Pita Chips*.

Yield: 2 cups (16 servings)

Nutrients per serving (2 tablespoons dip): Calories 60, Total Fat 5 g, Saturated Fat 1.5 g, Cholesterol 5 mg, Carbohydrate 2 g, Protein 2 g, Sodium 190 mg, Fiber less than 1 g

Diabetic exchanges per serving (2 tablespoons dip): 1 vegetable, 1 fat (0 carb)

BAKED PITA CHIPS

Prep time: 5 minutes • Bake time: 8-10 minutes per batch

Serve these light, crispy chips as dippers for warm, cheesy dips.

6   whole pita pocket bread rounds

1. Preheat oven to 400°F. Split each pita pocket in half horizontally; cut each round into eight wedges. Arrange half of the pita wedges in a single layer on **Large Round Stone**.

2. Bake 8-10 minutes or until chips are lightly browned and crisp. Remove from baking stone; cool completely. Repeat with remaining pita wedges.

Yield: 96 pita chips (12 servings)

Low Fat   Nutrients per serving (8 chips): Calories 80, Total Fat 0 g, Saturated Fat 0 g, Cholesterol 0 mg, Carbohydrate 17 g, Protein 3 g, Sodium 160 mg, Fiber less than 1 g

Diabetic exchanges per serving (8 chips): 1 starch (1 carb)

COOK'S TIPS

■ To thaw creamed spinach, cut a small slit in the center of the pouch. Microwave on 30% power 3 minutes or until thawed.

■ The Small Oval Baker is ideal for keeping hot dips and spreads warm while you and your guests enjoy the party.

■ When purchasing pita bread, be sure to buy pita bread rounds that have pockets so they can be split in half.

■ Use the **Pizza Cutter** to quickly and easily cut the pita rounds into even wedges.

- For best results, layer vegetables over the pizza in the order as directed in Step 3.

- Prebaking the pizza crust will help keep it from getting soggy when topped with vegetables that have a high water content.

- Sprinkling some of the cheese on the crust before topping the pizza provides a barrier between the crust and the moist toppings.

- Fresh zucchini is available year-round at most supermarkets. Select small zucchini, which are younger and more tender than the larger ones. Choose zucchini free of blemishes with a vibrant color.

- Italian seasoning can be substituted for the Italian Seasoning Mix, if desired.

THREE-CHEESE GARDEN PIZZA

Prep time: 20 minutes • Bake time: 22-25 minutes

Garden-fresh vegetables and a trio of cheeses make this pizza a winner. You can serve it as an appetizer or a light main dish.

1   package (10 ounces) refrigerated pizza crust
1   small onion, sliced into rings
1   medium zucchini, sliced
2   plum tomatoes, sliced
1   cup mushrooms, sliced
2   garlic cloves, pressed
1   cup (4 ounces) shredded mozzarella cheese
1   cup (4 ounces) shredded cheddar cheese
¼   cup (1 ounce) grated fresh Parmesan cheese
1   teaspoon **Pantry Italian Seasoning Mix**

1. Preheat oven to 400°F. Using lightly floured **Baker's Roller**™, roll pizza crust into a 14-inch circle on **Large Round Stone**. Bake crust 7 minutes. Remove from oven; place on **Stackable Cooling Rack**.

2. Using **Ultimate Slice & Grate** fitted with v-shaped blade, slice onion, zucchini and tomatoes. Slice mushrooms using **Egg Slicer Plus**®.

3. Using **Garlic Press**, press garlic over crust; spread evenly. Sprinkle mozzarella and cheddar cheeses evenly over crust; top evenly with onion, zucchini, mushrooms and tomatoes. Grate Parmesan cheese over vegetables using **Deluxe Cheese Grater**. Sprinkle with seasoning mix. Bake 15-18 minutes or until crust is golden brown; remove from oven. Cut into wedges.

Yield: 8 servings

Nutrients per serving: Calories 210, Total Fat 9 g, Saturated Fat 5 g, Cholesterol 25 mg, Carbohydrate 21 g, Protein 12 g, Sodium 450 mg, Fiber 1 g

Diabetic exchanges per serving: 1 starch, 1 vegetable, 1 meat, ½ fat (1 carb)

Fresh Salsa & Guacamole Duo

Prep time: 20 minutes • Stand time: 10 minutes

Side by side, this one-of-a-kind dip combo is a match made in heaven. A portion of the salsa is used to prepare the guacamole.

6 plum tomatoes, seeded and finely diced (1½ cups)
¼ cup finely chopped onion
¼ cup snipped fresh cilantro
1½ tablespoons fresh lime juice
½ teaspoon salt
⅛ teaspoon ground red pepper
2 firm, ripe avocados, peeled and diced
Baked Tortilla Chips (p. 19)

1. Finely dice tomatoes using **Chef's Knife**. Finely chop onion using **Food Chopper**. Place tomatoes and onion in **Classic Batter Bowl**. Add cilantro, lime juice, salt and ground red pepper to tomato mixture; mix gently. Let stand 10 minutes to allow flavors to blend.

2. Place avocados in **Small Batter Bowl**. Add ⅓ cup of the salsa mixture to avocados; mix gently. Spoon salsa and guacamole into small bowls. Serve with *Baked Tortilla Chips*.

Yield: 1½ cups salsa (12 servings)
1½ cups guacamole (12 servings)

Low Fat Nutrients per serving (2 tablespoons salsa): Calories 5, Total Fat 0 g, Saturated Fat 0 g, Cholesterol 0 mg, Carbohydrate 2 g, Protein 0 g, Sodium 80 g, Fiber 0 g

Diabetic exchanges per serving (2 tablespoons): Free food

Nutrients per serving (2 tablespoons guacamole): Calories 50, Total Fat 4 g, Saturated Fat 1 g, Cholesterol 0 mg, Carbohydrate 3 g, Protein 1 g, Sodium 20 mg, Fiber 3 g

Diabetic exchanges per serving (2 tablespoons): 1 fat (0 carb)

Fresh Salsa & Guacamole Duo, Baked Tortilla Chips (p. 19)

- Taco seasoning mix can be substituted for the Southwestern Seasoning Mix, if desired.

- For easier serving, arrange tomato slices over toppings in three rows of five.

- For a quick way to snip fresh herbs without the mess, place the herb in a small, deep bowl and snip with **Kitchen Shears**.

- This recipe can also be prepared in the **Stoneware Bar Pan**, if desired.

MEXICALI CORNBREAD SQUARES

Prep time: 25 minutes • Bake time: 12-15 minutes • Cool time: 45 minutes

These south-of-the-border appetizer squares are hot on flavor and easy to serve.

1 package (8.5 ounces) corn muffin mix (plus ingredients to make muffins)
1 egg
1 can (16 ounces) fat-free refried beans
1 tablespoon **Pantry Southwestern Seasoning Mix**
1 garlic clove, pressed
1 can (3.25 ounces) pitted ripe olives, drained and chopped
½ cup diced green bell pepper
2-3 plum tomatoes, sliced
½ cup (2 ounces) shredded cheddar cheese
1 container (8 ounces) sour cream
   Snipped fresh cilantro or parsley (optional)

1. Preheat oven to 350°F. Lightly spray **Rectangular Baker** with nonstick cooking spray. Prepare muffin mix according to package directions, adding additional egg. Pour batter into baker, spreading evenly. Bake 12-15 minutes or until **Cake Tester** inserted in center comes out clean. Remove from oven; cool completely.

2. In **Classic Batter Bowl**, combine refried beans, seasoning mix and garlic pressed with **Garlic Press**; mix well. Spread bean mixture over cornbread using **Large Spreader**. Chop olives using **Food Chopper**. Sprinkle olives and bell pepper over bean mixture. Arrange tomato slices evenly over toppings. Grate cheese over tomatoes using **Deluxe Cheese Grater**.

3. Attach open star tip to **Easy Accent®** **Decorator**; fill with sour cream. Pipe one rosette onto each tomato slice; sprinkle with cilantro. Cut into squares.

Yield: 15 servings

Nutrients per serving (1 square): Calories 210, Total Fat 9 g, Saturated Fat 4 g, Cholesterol 30 mg, Carbohydrate 28 g, Protein 6 g, Sodium 550 mg, Fiber 4 g

Diabetic exchanges per serving (1 square): 1½ starch, 2 fat (1½ carb)

NEW ORLEANS CRAB SPREAD

Prep time: 10 minutes • Chill time: 3 hours

Our Cajun Herb Seasoning Mix kicks the flavor up a notch in this light and simple spread.

4 ounces reduced-fat cream cheese (Neufchâtel), softened

½ cup fat-free mayonnaise

1 package (8 ounces) imitation crabmeat, chopped

¼ cup chopped celery

¼ cup chopped green bell pepper

1 garlic clove, pressed

1½ teaspoons **Pantry Cajun Herb Seasoning Mix**

Toasted Canapé Bread Slices (p. 45) or crackers

1. Place cream cheese in **Small Batter Bowl**. Microwave on HIGH 30 seconds or until softened; add mayonnaise and whisk until smooth. Chop crabmeat using **Food Chopper**. Chop celery and bell pepper using **Chef's Knife**.

2. Add crabmeat, celery, bell pepper, garlic pressed with **Garlic Press** and seasoning mix to cream cheese mixture; mix well. Cover; refrigerate 3 hours to allow flavors to blend. Serve with *Toasted Canapé Bread Slices* or crackers.

Yield: 2 cups (16 servings)

Low Fat Nutrients per serving (2 tablespoons): Calories 40, Total Fat 2 g, Saturated Fat 1 g, Cholesterol 10 mg, Carbohydrate 2 g, Protein 3 g, Sodium 125 mg, Fiber 0 g

Diabetic exchanges per serving (2 tablespoons): ½ meat (0 carb)

COOK'S TIPS

■ Cajun seasoning can be substituted for the Cajun Herb Seasoning Mix, if desired.

■ Imitation crabmeat (also known as surimi) is usually made from Alaskan pollock, a slightly sweet, lean fish. Surimi is available in the refrigerator or freezer section of most supermarkets. It can also be purchased in bulk at the fish counter.

New Orleans Crab Spread, Toasted Canapé Bread Slices (p. 45)

TEX-MEX CHICKEN MELTS

Prep time: 30 minutes • Bake time: 15-18 minutes

*These zesty appetizers are packed with flavor, thanks to our
Pantry Southwestern Seasoning Mix.*

1 loaf *Canapé French Bread* (p. 45)
1 can (10 ounces) chunk white chicken, drained and flaked
½ cup finely chopped onion
½ cup finely diced green bell pepper
1 cup (4 ounces) shredded cheddar cheese, divided
¼ cup mayonnaise
1 garlic clove, pressed
1 tablespoon **Pantry Southwestern Seasoning Mix**
¼ teaspoon salt
2 plum tomatoes, sliced
2 tablespoons snipped fresh cilantro or parsley

1. Preheat oven to 375°F. Slice bread into 20 slices, about ¼ inch thick. Arrange in a single layer on Rectangle Stone.

2. Place chicken in Classic Batter Bowl. Finely chop onion using Food Chopper. Add onion, bell pepper, ½ cup of the cheese, mayonnaise, garlic pressed with Garlic Press, seasoning mix and salt to batter bowl; mix well.

3. Using Medium Scoop, scoop chicken mixture evenly over bread slices; gently flatten filling with back of scoop. Using Ultimate Slice & Grate fitted with v-shaped blade, slice tomatoes. Top each bread slice with one tomato slice; sprinkle with remaining cheese.

4. Bake 15-18 minutes or until edges of bread are golden brown and cheese is melted. Remove from oven; sprinkle with cilantro. Serve warm.

Yield: 20 appetizers

Nutrients per serving (1 melt): Calories 110, Total Fat 6 g, Saturated Fat 2 g, Cholesterol 15 mg, Carbohydrate 8 g, Protein 6 g, Sodium 250 mg, Fiber 0 g

Diabetic exchanges per serving (1 melt): ½ starch, 1 meat (½ carb)

CHEESY ARTICHOKE TRIANGLES

Prep time: 25 minutes • Bake time: 35-42 minutes

Baked in our Stoneware Bar Pan, these savory, elegant pastry triangles are a perfect start to any special gathering.

2 packages (8 ounces each) refrigerated crescent rolls

2 packages (8 ounces each) cream cheese, softened

1 lemon

2 eggs

1 garlic clove, pressed

1 can (14 ounces) artichoke hearts in water, drained and finely chopped

1 cup (4 ounces) grated fresh Parmesan cheese, divided

2 plum tomatoes, sliced

2 tablespoons snipped fresh parsley

½ teaspoon coarsely ground black pepper

1. Preheat oven to 375°F. Unroll one package of crescent rolls across one end of **Stoneware Bar Pan** with longest sides of dough across width of pan. Repeat with remaining package of dough, filling pan. Using **Baker's Roller™**, roll dough to seal perforations and press up sides to form crust. Bake 10-12 minutes or until light golden brown. Remove from oven.

2. Meanwhile, place cream cheese in **Classic Batter Bowl**; whisk until smooth. Zest lemon using **Lemon Zester/Scorer** to measure 1 teaspoon zest. Add lemon zest, eggs and garlic pressed with **Garlic Press** to cream cheese; mix well. Finely chop artichokes with **Food Chopper**. Grate Parmesan cheese using **Deluxe Cheese Grater**. Add artichokes and ½ cup of the Parmesan cheese to cream cheese mixture; mix well.

3. Spread artichoke mixture evenly over crust; arrange tomato slices over filling. Combine remaining Parmesan cheese, parsley and black pepper in **Small Batter Bowl**; sprinkle cheese mixture evenly over filling. Bake 25-30 minutes or until light golden brown and set. Remove from oven; cool 10 minutes. Cut into 12 squares; cut each square in half diagonally.

Yield: 24 appetizers

Nutrients per serving (1 triangle): Calories 170, Total Fat 12 g, Saturated Fat 6 g, Cholesterol 40 mg, Carbohydrate 10 g, Protein 5 g, Sodium 300 mg, Fiber less than 1 g

Diabetic exchanges per serving (1 triangle): 1 starch, 2 fat (1 carb)

COOK'S TIPS

- To soften both packages of cream cheese, microwave on HIGH 60 seconds or until softened.

- The **Ultimate Slice & Grate** is a versatile tool with four different blades for slicing and grating. Use the v-shaped blade to easily slice the tomatoes into uniform ¼-inch-thick slices.

SAUCY SEAFOOD PIZZA

Prep time: 30 minutes • Bake time: 14-17 minutes • Cool time: 45 minutes

A flaky crescent roll crust topped with cream cheese, cocktail sauce, crunchy vegetables and crabmeat is a winning flavor combination.

1 package (8 ounces) refrigerated crescent rolls
1 package (8 ounces) cream cheese, softened
1 teaspoon **Pantry All-Purpose Dill Mix**
1 lemon
½ cup seafood cocktail sauce
4 ounces imitation crabmeat, coarsely chopped
½ medium cucumber, seeded, sliced and quartered
¼ cup diced green bell pepper
1 tablespoon snipped fresh parsley

1. Preheat oven to 350°F. Unroll crescent dough; separate into eight triangles. On **Classic Round Stone**, arrange triangles in a circle with points in the center and wide ends toward the outside. Using lightly floured **Baker's Roller**™, roll out dough to a 12-inch circle, pressing seams together to seal. Bake 14-17 minutes or until light golden brown. Remove from oven; cool completely.

2. In **Small Batter Bowl**, combine cream cheese and dill mix. Zest lemon using **Lemon Zester/Scorer** to measure 1 teaspoon zest; add to cream cheese mixture and mix well. Spread cream cheese mixture evenly over crust; spread evenly with cocktail sauce.

3. Coarsely chop crabmeat using **Food Chopper**. Cut cucumber in half crosswise; remove seeds. Slice cucumber using **Ultimate Slice & Grate**; cut slices into quarters. Dice bell pepper using **Chef's Knife**. Top pizza with crabmeat, cucumber and bell pepper; sprinkle with parsley. Refrigerate 30 minutes. Cut into wedges.

Yield: 10 servings

Nutrients per serving: Calories 200, Total Fat 13 g, Saturated Fat 6 g, Cholesterol 25 mg, Carbohydrate 14 g, Protein 5 g, Sodium 510 mg, Fiber 0 g

Diabetic exchanges per serving: 1 starch, 2½ fat (1 carb)

MUSHROOM FOCACCIA BREAD

Prep and cook time: 25 minutes • Bake time: 25-30 minutes

This savory bread, accented by our Rosemary Herb Seasoning Mix, tastes as good as it smells.

16 ounces mushrooms, sliced

1 cup chopped onion

1 pouch (16 ounces) **Pantry Pizza Crust & Roll Mix** (including yeast packet)

1 tablespoon plus 1 teaspoon **Pantry Rosemary Herb Seasoning Mix,** divided

1¼ cups very warm water (120°F-130°F)

2 tablespoons olive or vegetable oil

¼ cup reduced-fat mayonnaise

2 garlic cloves, pressed

¾ cup (3 ounces) grated fresh Parmesan cheese, divided

1. Preheat oven to 400°F. Slice mushrooms using **Egg Slicer Plus**®. Chop onion using **Food Chopper**. Heat **Stir-Fry Skillet** over high heat; lightly spray with vegetable oil using **Kitchen Spritzer**. Add mushrooms and onion; cook, stirring frequently, 5-7 minutes or until mushrooms are golden brown and all liquid is absorbed. Remove from heat; set aside.

2. In **Classic Batter Bowl**, combine pizza crust mix, yeast packet and 1 tablespoon of the seasoning mix. Add water and oil; stir until mixture forms a ball. Turn dough out onto well-floured surface. With floured hands, gently knead dough 8-10 times. Lightly sprinkle **Rectangle Stone** with flour. Roll dough to edges of baking stone using lightly floured **Baker's Roller**.™

3. In **Small Batter Bowl**, combine mayonnaise, garlic pressed with **Garlic Press** and remaining seasoning mix; mix well. Spread mayonnaise mixture evenly over dough to within ½ inch of edge.

4. Grate Parmesan cheese using **Deluxe Cheese Grater**. Sprinkle ½ cup of the cheese over mayonnaise mixture. Spoon mushroom mixture evenly over mayonnaise mixture. Sprinkle with remaining cheese. Bake 25-30 minutes or until crust is golden brown. Remove from oven. Cut into squares; serve warm.

Yield: 12 servings

Nutrients per serving: Calories 210, Total Fat 7 g, Saturated Fat 2 g, Cholesterol 5 mg, Carbohydrate 32 g, Protein 8 g, Sodium 280 mg, Fiber 2 g

Diabetic exchanges per serving: 2 starch, 1 fat (2 carb)

COOK'S TIPS

- The Egg Slicer Plus works best with firm, fresh mushrooms. Wipe mushrooms clean with a damp paper towel and trim off stem ends. Place mushroom stem end up in the egg slicer and slice.

- When making pizzas and pies, you'll find our Baker's Roller is easier to use than a traditional rolling pin. It is designed for one-handed use, and the compact rollers allow you to roll dough right on flat baking stones and bakers.

- One package (16 ounces) hot roll mix can be substituted for the Pizza Crust & Roll Mix, if desired.

- Crushed dried rosemary leaves can be substituted for the Rosemary Herb Seasoning Mix, if desired.

LEMON PEPPER CRAB CANAPÉS

Prep time: 15 minutes

Perfect for a brunch or shower, these light, attractive canapés are impressive and easy to make.

■ To keep the bread slices from becoming soggy, remove the seeds from the cucumber with **The Corer**™.

■ Save time on the day of the party by baking the *Canapé French Bread* a day in advance. Store the cooled bread in a resealable plastic food storage bag to keep it fresh. Slice the bread just before you're ready to assemble the canapés.

■ You can make the crab mixture several hours in advance and keep it refrigerated in the covered batter bowl until you're ready to use it.

1 loaf *Canapé French Bread* (p. 45)
1 package (8 ounces) imitation crabmeat, coarsely chopped
1 can (8 ounces) sliced water chestnuts, drained and chopped
1 small carrot, grated (about ¼ cup)
1 lemon
1 green onion with top, thinly sliced
⅓ cup reduced-fat mayonnaise
½ teaspoon coarsely ground black pepper
1 medium cucumber, scored, seeded and sliced
Fresh parsley leaves (optional)

1. Slice bread into twenty-four ¼-inch-thick slices; arrange in a single layer on serving platter.

2. Coarsely chop crabmeat and water chestnuts using **Food Chopper**; place in **Classic Batter Bowl**. Grate carrot using **Deluxe Cheese Grater**. Zest lemon with **Lemon Zester/Scorer** to measure 1 tablespoon zest. Juice lemon to measure 1 tablespoon juice. Add carrot, lemon zest, juice, green onion, mayonnaise and black pepper to batter bowl; mix well.

3. Score cucumber lengthwise using Lemon/Zester Scorer. Cut cucumber in half crosswise; remove seeds. Using **Ultimate Slice & Grate** fitted with v-shaped blade, slice cucumber. Top each bread slice with one cucumber slice. Using **Small Scoop**, scoop crab mixture evenly over cucumber slices. Garnish with fresh parsley, if desired. Serve immediately.

Yield: 24 servings

Low Fat Nutrients per serving (1 canapé):
Calories 60, Total Fat 1.5 g, Saturated Fat 0 g, Cholesterol less than 5 mg, Carbohydrate 8 g, Protein 2 g, Sodium 190 mg, Fiber less than 1 g

Diabetic exchanges per serving (1 canapé): ½ starch (½ carb)

ORIENTAL VEGETABLE PIZZA

Prep time: 20 minutes • Bake time: 8-10 minutes • Cool time: 30 minutes

*If you are bored by lackluster pizzas, this meatless wonder will widen your horizons.
As an added bonus, it's low fat!*

1   package (10 ounces) thin prebaked
    pizza crust

1   package (8 ounces) fat-free cream
    cheese, softened

1   teaspoon reduced-sodium soy sauce

1   garlic clove, pressed

1   1/2-inch piece peeled fresh gingerroot,
    pressed

1/2   cup *each:* diced red bell pepper,
      broccoli florets, sliced snow peas
      and grated carrot

1/4   cup sweet and sour sauce
      Fresh cilantro leaves (optional)

1. Preheat oven to 450°F. Place pizza crust on
   Classic Round Stone; bake 8-10 minutes
   or until crisp. Remove from oven; cool
   completely.

2. Combine cream cheese and soy sauce in
   Small Batter Bowl. Add garlic and
   gingerroot pressed with **Garlic Press**; mix
   well. Spread cream cheese mixture evenly
   over top of crust.

3. Dice bell pepper and cut broccoli into
   florets using **Chef's Knife**. Slice snow peas
   lengthwise into thin strips. Grate carrot
   using **Ultimate Slice & Grate**. Top pizza
   with vegetables. Drizzle with sweet and
   sour sauce. Garnish with cilantro,
   if desired.

Yield: 10 servings

Low Fat   Nutrients per serving: Calories 110, Total Fat 2 g,
            Saturated Fat .5 g, Cholesterol less than 5 mg,
Carbohydrate 18 g, Protein 7 g, Sodium 320 mg, Fiber 1 g

Diabetic exchanges per serving: 1 starch, 1/2 meat (1 carb)

GAME DAY PARTY MIX

Prep time: 15 minutes • Bake time: 20 minutes • Stand time: 10-15 minutes

This crunchy, savory treat signals the start of football festivities.
So sit back, relax and enjoy the game!

4   cups crispy corn and rice cereal

2   cups miniature pretzel twists

1   cup fish-shaped cheddar cheese
    crackers

¼   cup butter or margarine, melted

1   small garlic clove, pressed

¼   cup (1 ounce) grated fresh Parmesan
    cheese

1   package (0.4 ounce) buttermilk
    recipe ranch salad dressing mix

1   package (3-3.5 ounces) microwave
    popcorn

1. Preheat oven to 350°F. In **Stoneware Baking Bowl**, combine cereal, pretzels and crackers; mix gently. Place butter in **Small Micro-Cooker®**; microwave on HIGH 45 seconds or until melted. Press garlic into butter using **Garlic Press**. Pour butter mixture over cereal mixture, stirring to coat evenly.

2. Grate Parmesan cheese over cereal mixture using **Deluxe Cheese Grater**; mix gently. Sprinkle with dressing mix; mix gently to coat evenly.

3. Bake 20 minutes. Remove baking bowl from oven. Prepare popcorn according to package directions. Carefully stir popcorn into warm cereal mixture. Let stand in baking bowl 10-15 minutes before serving.

Yield: 16 cups (16 servings)

Nutrients per serving (1 cup): Calories 130, Total Fat 6 g, Saturated Fat 3 g, Cholesterol 10 mg, Carbohydrate 17 g, Protein 3 g, Sodium 320 mg, Fiber 1 g

Diabetic exchanges per serving (1 cup): 1 starch, 1 fat (1 carb)

Game Day Party Mix, Garden Dip (p. 44)

GARDEN DIP

Prep time: 10 minutes

Serve this creamy dip with your favorite vegetable dippers for a fresh snack.

- To easily seed a tomato, cut it in half crosswise. Hold the tomato halves cut sides down and gently squeeze to release the seeds and watery pulp.

- To make cucumber-carrot slices, cut a cucumber in half crosswise. Remove seeds using **The Corer.™** Insert a peeled carrot into the center of the cucumber; slice with the **Crinkle Cutter.**

- To make celery fans, cut celery into 3- to 4-inch pieces. Open the **Egg Slicer Plus®** and push one end of the celery halfway through the wires. Remove; turn the celery one-fourth of a turn and push halfway through wires. Repeat with opposite end of the celery. Place the celery fan in ice water until the ends curl.

- For an interesting ridged effect, use the Crinkle Cutter to cut vegetables such as carrots, jicama or zucchini into spears or slices.

1 package (8 ounces) cream cheese, softened
2 tablespoons mayonnaise
1 teaspoon **Pantry All-Purpose Dill Mix**
1 garlic clove, pressed
1 plum tomato, seeded and diced
¼ cup diced green bell pepper
1 small carrot, finely grated (about ¼ cup)
   Salt and ground black pepper to taste
1-2 tablespoons milk
1 large red bell pepper
   Assorted fresh vegetable dippers

1. In **Small Batter Bowl**, combine cream cheese, mayonnaise, dill mix and garlic pressed with **Garlic Press**; mix well. Dice tomato and green bell pepper using **Chef's Knife**. Grate carrot using **Deluxe Cheese Grater**. Add vegetables to cream cheese mixture; mix well. Season to taste with salt and black pepper. Add 1-2 tablespoons milk to dip to adjust consistency.

2. Using **V-Shaped Cutter**, cut off top of red bell pepper. Discard top, membranes and seeds. Place bell pepper in center of serving platter; fill with dip. Serve with assorted vegetables.

Yield: 1½ cups dip (12 servings)

Nutrients per serving (2 tablespoons dip): Calories 90, Total Fat 9 g, Saturated Fat 4 g, Cholesterol 20 mg, Carbohydrate 2 g, Protein 2 g, Sodium 100 mg, Fiber 0 g

Diabetic exchanges per serving (2 tablespoons dip): ½ vegetable, 2 fat (0 carb)

Variation: *Guilt-Free Garden Dip:* Substitute fat-free cream cheese and fat-free mayonnaise for cream cheese and mayonnaise. Omit milk.

Low Fat   Nutrients per serving (2 tablespoons dip): Calories 25, Total Fat 0 g, Saturated Fat 0 g, Cholesterol less than 5 mg, Carbohydrate 2 g, Protein 3 g, Sodium 135 mg, Fiber 0 g

Diabetic exchanges per serving (2 tablespoons dip): Free food

CANAPÉ FRENCH BREAD

Prep and bake time: 50-60 minutes • Cool time: 1 hour

This shaped cocktail bread can be used for a wide variety of appetizers.

1 package (11 ounces) refrigerated
   French bread dough

1. Preheat oven to 375°F. Lightly spray inside of **Scalloped Bread Tube** and lids with nonstick cooking spray. Place lid on bottom of bread tube; fill tube with dough. Place lid on top. Bake, upright, 50-60 minutes. Remove from oven; cool 10 minutes.

2. Remove bread from tube; cool completely. Cut bread into ¼-inch-thick slices with **Serrated Bread Knife.**

Yield: 24 slices (1 loaf)

Low Fat Nutrients per serving (2 slices):
Calories 60, Total Fat 1 g, Saturated Fat 0 g, Cholesterol 0 mg, Carbohydrate 11 g, Protein 2 g, Sodium 160 mg, Fiber 0 g

Diabetic exchanges per serving (2 slices): 1 starch (1 carb)

Variation: *Toasted Canapé Bread Slices*
(Pictured on p. 28): To toast canapé bread slices, preheat oven to 350°F. Arrange slices in a single layer on **Rectangle Stone.** Bake 10-12 minutes or until light golden brown. Cool completely.

(Pictured on p. 28)

COOK'S TIPS

■ The Scalloped Bread Tube can be used as a large cookie cutter. You can also use it to cut out crisp rice cereal treats. Spray the tube with a little nonstick cooking spray to avoid sticking.

■ For sandwiches that are fun to eat, simply assemble sandwich ingredients as usual and cut out the center with the Scalloped Bread Tube. Crusts get cut off, and the sandwich is instantly transformed into a neat shape!

Let's Get
TOGETHER

Dinner, lunch...
and even
brunch.

Savory Sandwich Ring (p. 48),
Summer Tortellini Salad (p. 49)

- The bread ring can be baked up to 1 day ahead of time. Cool it completely and wrap it securely in plastic wrap.

- Italian seasoning can be substituted for the Italian Seasoning Mix, if desired.

SAVORY SANDWICH RING

Prep time: 30 minutes • Bake time: 26-30 minutes • Cool time: 1 hour

Herbed French bread forms the base for this hearty sandwich layered with your choice of deli meats, cheeses and crispy vegetables. (Pictured on p. 46-47)

2 packages (11 ounces each) refrigerated French bread dough

1 egg white, lightly beaten

3 garlic cloves, pressed

1 teaspoon **Pantry Italian Seasoning Mix**

1 medium green bell pepper, thinly sliced

1 medium onion, thinly sliced

1 medium tomato, thinly sliced

1/2 cup pitted ripe olives, sliced

8 ounces thinly sliced deli meat, such as hard salami, turkey, ham or bologna

4 ounces thinly sliced cheese, such as Swiss, Muenster or American

2 cups thinly sliced lettuce

1/4 cup plus 2 tablespoons Italian salad dressing, divided

1. Preheat oven to 350°F. Place dough, seam side down, on **Large Round Stone**. Join ends of dough together to form one large ring. Using **Serrated Bread Knife**, make eight diagonal cuts, 1/2 inch deep, on top of dough.

2. Combine egg white, garlic pressed with **Garlic Press** and seasoning mix; brush over dough using **Pastry Brush**. Bake 26-30 minutes or until deep golden brown. Immediately remove bread to **Stackable Cooling Rack**; cool completely.

3. Using **Ultimate Slice & Grate** fitted with v-shaped blade, slice bell pepper, onion and tomato. Slice olives using **Egg Slicer Plus®**.

4. To assemble sandwich, cut bread in half horizontally using Serrated Bread Knife. Place bottom half of bread on large serving platter. Arrange meat and cheese evenly over bottom half of bread. Top with lettuce. Drizzle 2 tablespoons of the salad dressing evenly over lettuce. Top with bell pepper, onion, tomato and olive slices. Brush cut side of bread top with remaining dressing using clean Pastry Brush; place over bottom half. Cut into wedges.

Yield: 8 servings

Nutrients per serving: Calories 380, Total Fat 16 g, Saturated Fat 7 g, Cholesterol 35 mg, Carbohydrate 40 g, Protein 18 g, Sodium 1240 mg, Fiber 2 g

Diabetic exchanges per serving: 2 1/2 starch, 1 1/2 meat, 1 fat (2 1/2 carb)

SUMMER TORTELLINI SALAD

Prep time: 20 minutes • Cook time: 7-9 minutes • Chill time: 2 hours

Serve this simple, colorful salad at your next outdoor gathering. (Pictured on p. 46-47)

1 package (9 ounces) uncooked refrigerated cheese-filled tortellini
1 medium zucchini, thinly sliced
1 large carrot, peeled and chopped
1 pint cherry tomatoes, halved
4 green onions with tops, thinly sliced
¼ cup snipped fresh parsley
½ cup fat-free ranch salad dressing
2 tablespoons grated fresh Parmesan cheese

1. Cook tortellini according to package directions in **Professional (8-qt.) Stockpot**; drain and rinse under cold running water. Place pasta in large **Colander Bowl** and set aside.

2. Meanwhile, slice zucchini using **Ultimate Slice & Grate** fitted with v-shaped blade. Chop carrot using **Food Chopper**. Cut cherry tomatoes in half and thinly slice green onions. Snip parsley using **Kitchen Shears**.

3. Add vegetables to tortellini. Pour salad dressing over salad. Grate Parmesan cheese over salad using **Deluxe Cheese Grater**; mix gently. Cover; refrigerate at least 2 hours before serving.

Yield: 6 servings

Low Fat   Nutrients per serving (1 cup): Calories 180, Total Fat 3 g, Saturated Fat 1.5 g, Cholesterol 15 mg, Carbohydrate 31 g, Protein 7 g, Sodium 490 mg, Fiber 3 g

Diabetic exchanges per serving (1 cup): 2 starch (2 carb)

COOK'S TIPS

- This recipe can be easily doubled. Use a 20-ounce package of uncooked refrigerated cheese-filled tortellini or a 19-ounce package of uncooked frozen cheese-filled tortellini.

- When making pasta salads, it's a good idea to rinse the cooked pasta under cold running water to wash off the starch and keep the pasta from sticking together.

- The cooking time for fresh pasta is shorter than for dried pasta, so follow the package directions carefully.

FABULOUS FAJITA PIZZA

Prep time: 40 minutes • Bake time: 18-22 minutes • Stand time: 10 minutes

Fajitas become a new-fangled, one-dish favorite when you stir-fry topping ingredients and bake them on a pizza crust.

1 medium green bell pepper

1 medium red bell pepper

1 medium onion

2 boneless, skinless chicken breast halves (about 4 ounces each)

2 packages (10 ounces each) refrigerated pizza crust

1 teaspoon vegetable oil, divided

1-2 teaspoons **Pantry Southwestern Seasoning Mix**

1 garlic clove, pressed

¼ cup thick and chunky salsa

2 cups (8 ounces) shredded Colby & Monterey Jack cheese blend, divided

2 tablespoons snipped fresh cilantro

Additional thick and chunky salsa and sour cream (optional)

1. Preheat oven to 425°F. Cut bell peppers into ½-inch-thick strips using **Utility Knife**. Cut onion into ½-inch-thick wedges. Cut chicken crosswise into thin strips.

2. Lightly sprinkle **Large Round Stone** with flour using **Flour/Sugar Shaker**. Unroll both packages of pizza dough and arrange side by side on baking stone, shaping into a circle. Using lightly floured **Baker's Roller™**, roll dough to edge of baking stone, pressing seams to seal.

3. Heat **Stir-Fry Skillet** over high heat. Add ½ teaspoon of the oil and chicken; stir-fry 2-3 minutes or until chicken is no longer pink. Remove from skillet. Add remaining oil, bell peppers, onion and seasoning mix to skillet. Press garlic over vegetables using **Garlic Press**. Stir-fry 1-2 minutes or until vegetables are crisp-tender. Remove skillet from heat; stir in chicken and salsa.

4. Sprinkle half of the cheese evenly over crust. Arrange chicken mixture over cheese. Sprinkle remaining cheese over chicken mixture.

5. Bake 18-22 minutes or until crust is golden brown. Remove from oven. Sprinkle cilantro over pizza; let stand 10 minutes. Cut into wedges. Serve with additional salsa and sour cream, if desired.

Yield: 8 servings

Nutrients per serving: Calories 350, Total Fat 12 g, Saturated Fat 6 g, Cholesterol 45 mg, Carbohydrate 38 g, Protein 20 g, Sodium 720 mg, Fiber 2 g

Diabetic exchanges per serving: 2½ starch, 2 meat (2½ carb)

- You can omit the chicken for a meatless version of this pizza, if desired.

- If desired, 1 teaspoon chili powder and ½ teaspoon ground cumin can be substituted for the Southwestern Seasoning Mix.

- Mexican cheese blend can be substituted for the Colby & Monterey Jack cheese blend, if desired.

- Use the **Chef's Knife** to cut the pizza into wedges; serve using the **Large Serving Spatula**.

ASIAN LETTUCE ROLLS

Prep time: 1 hour • Microwave time: 8-10 minutes

This restaurant-style entrée looks stunning when presented on our Simple Additions™ serving pieces.

2 packages (3 ounces each) chicken-flavor ramen noodles

2 cups coarsely chopped cooked chicken

1 *each:* red and yellow bell pepper

½ cup thinly sliced green onions with tops

2 tablespoons reduced-sodium soy sauce

2 teaspoons **Pantry Asian Seasoning Mix**

2 teaspoons vegetable oil

1 garlic clove, pressed

1 ½-inch piece peeled fresh gingerroot, pressed

1 medium cucumber, scored, seeded and thinly sliced

2 medium carrots, peeled and cut into julienne strips

¼ cup chopped peanuts (optional)

24 Boston lettuce leaves

1 jar (11.5 ounces) sweet and sour sauce

1. In **Large Micro-Cooker®**, microwave 3 cups water on HIGH 6-8 minutes or until boiling. Break each block of noodles into quarters; add noodles and seasoning packets to boiling water. Microwave, covered, 2 minutes; stir. Drain noodles and rinse under cold water.

2. Coarsely chop chicken with **Food Chopper**. Slice tops and bottoms off bell peppers; remove stems and chop tops and bottoms of bell peppers. Set center portions of bell peppers aside. Place noodles, chicken, chopped bell peppers and green onions in **Classic Batter Bowl**.

3. In **Small Batter Bowl**, combine soy sauce, seasoning mix and oil. Add garlic and ginger pressed with **Garlic Press**. Pour over noodle mixture in batter bowl; toss to coat. Cover and refrigerate.

4. Slice reserved bell peppers into thin strips. Using **Ultimate Slice & Grate**, thinly slice cucumber. Cut carrots into julienne strips using **Julienne Peeler**. To serve, spoon noodle salad into medium bowl; sprinkle with peanuts, if desired. Place bell peppers, cucumber, carrots and sweet and sour sauce into small bowls. To serve, top each lettuce leaf with noodle salad and vegetables. Drizzle with sweet and sour sauce and roll up.

Yield: 8 servings

Nutrients per serving (3 rolls): Calories 190, Total Fat 3.5 g, Saturated Fat 1 g, Cholesterol 30 mg, Carbohydrate 27 g, Protein 12 g, Sodium 400 mg, Fiber 2 g

Diabetic exchanges per serving (3 rolls): 1½ starch, 1 meat (1½ carb)

BISTRO CHICKEN TWIST

Prep time: 20 minutes • Bake time: 30-32 minutes

Fresh basil accents this delightful stuffed bread. Serve it for lunch with a salad of mixed greens.

1 cup chopped cooked chicken

½ cup diced red bell pepper

¼ cup snipped fresh basil leaves

¼ cup plus 2 tablespoons (1½ ounces) grated fresh Parmesan cheese, divided

½ cup (2 ounces) shredded mozzarella cheese

¼ cup mayonnaise

1 garlic clove, pressed

2 packages (11 ounces each) refrigerated French bread dough

1 egg white, lightly beaten

1 teaspoon **Pantry Italian Seasoning Mix**

1. Preheat oven to 375°F. Chop chicken using **Food Chopper**. Dice bell pepper using **Chef's Knife**. Snip basil using **Kitchen Shears**. In **Classic Batter Bowl**, combine chicken, bell pepper, basil, ¼ cup of the Parmesan cheese, mozzarella cheese, mayonnaise and garlic pressed with **Garlic Press**; mix well.

2. Place bread dough, seam sides up, on smooth side of **Large Grooved Cutting Board**. Using **Serrated Bread Knife**, slice each loaf lengthwise, end to end, cutting halfway through to center of loaf; spread open flat. Lightly sprinkle flour evenly over dough. Using **Baker's Roller**™, roll dough crosswise to a 4-inch width, creating a well down center of each loaf.

3. Spoon half of the chicken mixture down center of each loaf. Gather up edges over filling, pinching firmly to seal. Place loaves, seam sides down, in an "X" pattern on **Rectangle Stone**. Crisscross ends of dough to form a large figure "8," keeping ends of dough 1 inch from edge of stone and leaving two 1½-inch openings in center of twist.

4. Combine egg white and seasoning mix; lightly brush over dough. Cut a 3-inch slit in each of the top sections of the twist to reveal filling. Sprinkle remaining 2 tablespoons Parmesan cheese over loaf. Bake 30-32 minutes or until deep golden brown. Remove from oven; cool 10 minutes.

Yield: 8 servings

Nutrients per serving: Calories 300, Total Fat 10 g, Saturated Fat 3 g, Cholesterol 20 mg, Carbohydrate 38 g, Protein 15 g, Sodium 650 mg, Fiber 0 g

Diabetic exchanges per serving: 2½ starch, 1 meat, ½ fat (2½ carb)

Variation: *Pepperoni Pizza Twist* (Pictured at right): For filling, combine 1 package (3.5 ounces) pepperoni slices, diced, 1 can (3.25 ounces) pitted ripe olives, drained and chopped, ½ cup (2 ounces) shredded mozzarella cheese, 2 tablespoons snipped fresh parsley, 2 tablespoons all-purpose flour and 1 pressed garlic clove. Continue as recipe directs in Steps 2 through 4. Sprinkle the loaf with 2 tablespoons grated fresh Parmesan cheese before baking.

Lightly sprinkle flour evenly over dough. Roll dough crosswise to a 4-inch width, creating a well down center of each loaf.

Spoon half of the filling down center of each loaf. Gather up edges over filling, pinching firmly to seal.

Place loaves, seam sides down, in an "X" pattern on baking stone. Crisscross ends of dough to form a figure "8."

SPRING PASTA STIR-FRY

Prep time: 25 minutes • Cook time: 15-17 minutes

This colorful stir-fry is a light main-dish meal, just right for any night of the week.

1 package (12 ounces) uncooked fettuccini noodles

1 large carrot, peeled and cut into julienne strips

1 small yellow summer squash, cut into julienne strips

1 small zucchini, cut into julienne strips

3 plum tomatoes, seeded and cut into strips

2 tablespoons olive oil, divided

2 garlic cloves, pressed

3/4 teaspoon salt, divided

1/4 cup snipped fresh basil leaves

1/4 teaspoon coarsely ground black pepper

1 ounce shaved fresh Parmesan cheese

1. In **Professional (8-qt.) Stockpot**, cook pasta according to package directions; drain. Return pasta to stockpot; keep warm.

2. Meanwhile, prepare vegetables. Using **Julienne Peeler**, cut carrot, yellow squash and zucchini into long julienne strips. Slice tomatoes in half lengthwise and remove seeds using **Cook's Corer™**; slice tomatoes into 1/4-inch strips.

3. Heat **Stir-Fry Skillet** over medium heat. Add 1 tablespoon of the oil and garlic pressed with **Garlic Press**; cook and stir 2-3 minutes or until garlic is softened and begins to brown. Add carrot, yellow squash, zucchini, tomatoes and 1/4 teaspoon of the salt; stir-fry 1-2 minutes or until vegetables are crisp-tender.

4. Add remaining oil, remaining salt, basil and black pepper to pasta; toss gently. To serve, spoon pasta into serving bowl; top with vegetable mixture. Sprinkle with Parmesan cheese. Serve immediately.

Yield: 8 servings

Nutrients per serving: Calories 180, Total Fat 5 g, Saturated Fat 1 g, Cholesterol 0 mg, Carbohydrate 26 g, Protein 7 g, Sodium 360 mg, Fiber 2 g

Diabetic exchanges per serving: 1 1/2 starch, 1/2 vegetable, 1 fat (1 1/2 carb)

COOK'S TIPS

- For a special touch, slice basil leaves into thin ribbons or strips called "chiffonade" [shif-un-NAHD]. Stack the basil leaves and roll them up into a tight cylinder. Using the **Chef's Knife**, slice the roll crosswise into thin strips. This technique can be used for lettuce leaves as well.

- Use the **Vegetable Peeler** to shave the Parmesan cheese into thin pieces.

- For a heartier main dish, 2 cooked chicken breast halves, cut into 1/4-inch strips, can be added to the vegetable mixture, if desired.

- Place 2- to 3-inch-wide strips of aluminum foil over tips of bread if they begin to brown too much.

- Store ripe tomatoes, stem side down, at room temperature away from direct sunlight. Refrigerating tomatoes makes them mealy and tends to destroy their flavor.

- To make bacon slices come apart more easily, roll the package into a tube and secure it with a rubber band before refrigerating. It also helps to remove the bacon from the refrigerator up to 30 minutes before cooking.

DEEP DISH BLT PIZZA

Prep time: 30 minutes • Bake time: 35-40 minutes • Stand time: 10 minutes

The all-time favorite flavor combination of bacon, lettuce and tomato blooms like a flower in our Deep Dish Baker.

2 packages (11 ounces each) refrigerated bread sticks

1 cup (4 ounces) shredded mozzarella cheese, divided

4 ounces sliced deli turkey breast, coarsely chopped

4 slices bacon, crisply cooked, drained and crumbled

1/3 cup thinly sliced green onions with tops

2 plum tomatoes, sliced

2 cups thinly sliced romaine lettuce

2 tablespoons ranch dressing

1. Preheat oven to 350°F. Separate one package of the bread stick dough; separate into strips. Arrange strips in a spiral pattern to completely line bottom of **Deep Dish Baker**. Using lightly floured **Baker's Roller™**, roll dough to seal seams.

2. Slice remaining package of dough lengthwise in half using **Serrated Bread Knife**. Lay each half, flat side down, and slice crosswise into 12 half moons for a total of 24 pieces. Form a decorative edge by arranging pieces of dough next to each other, standing on end, against sides of baker. Use Baker's Roller to seal bottom edge of dough pieces to base.

3. Sprinkle half of the cheese evenly over dough. Coarsely chop turkey using **Food Chopper**; place in **Small Batter Bowl**. Add bacon and green onions; mix well. Spread turkey mixture over cheese.

4. Slice tomatoes into 1/4-inch-thick slices; arrange over filling. Sprinkle with remaining cheese. Bake 35-40 minutes or until edges of bread are deep golden brown. Remove pizza from oven; let stand 10 minutes. Arrange lettuce around outer edge of pizza; drizzle with dressing.

Yield: 8 servings

Nutrients per serving: Calories 310, Total Fat 10 g, Saturated Fat 2.5 g, Cholesterol 15 mg, Carbohydrate 41 g, Protein 14 g, Sodium 910 mg, Fiber 2 g

Diabetic exchanges per serving: 2½ starch, 1 meat, ½ fat (2½ carb)

CAJUN CHILI CORNBREAD SKILLET

Prep time: 20 minutes • Bake time: 30-35 minutes

Gather around the dinner table and turn out a winner with this satisfying main dish meal the whole family will enjoy.

1 pound lean (93%) ground turkey

1 can (15-15½ ounces) chili beans in sauce

2 tablespoons **Pantry Cajun Herb Seasoning Mix**, divided

1 garlic clove, pressed

1 red bell pepper, sliced into rings

1 green bell pepper, sliced into rings

¾ cup chopped onion

2 packages (8.5 ounces each) corn muffin mix

1 cup (4 ounces) shredded sharp cheddar cheese, divided

½ cup water

3 eggs

1. Preheat oven to 350°F. In **Family (12-in.) Skillet**, cook and stir ground turkey over medium heat 8-10 minutes or until no longer pink; drain if necessary. In medium bowl, combine turkey, chili beans, 1 tablespoon of the seasoning mix and garlic pressed with **Garlic Press**.

2. Using **Chef's Knife**, slice six ¼-inch-thick rings from each bell pepper for a total of 12 rings. Arrange bell pepper rings in an overlapping circular pattern over bottom of skillet. Chop onion using **Food Chopper**; sprinkle over bell peppers. Carefully spoon turkey mixture over vegetables in skillet.

3. In **Classic Batter Bowl**, combine muffin mixes, remaining seasoning mix and half of the cheese; mix well. Add water and eggs; mix well. Pour batter evenly over turkey mixture. Bake, uncovered, 30-35 minutes or until **Cake Tester** inserted in center comes out clean.

4. Using **Oven Mitts**, carefully remove skillet from oven. Loosen edges of cornbread from skillet. Carefully invert cornbread onto large, heat-safe serving plate. Sprinkle with remaining cheese. Cut into wedges and serve using **Slice 'N Serve®**.

Yield: 12 servings

Nutrients per serving: Calories 310, Total Fat 10 g, Saturated Fat 4 g, Cholesterol 90 mg, Carbohydrate 18 g, Protein 15 g, Sodium 320 mg, Fiber 4 g

Diabetic exchanges per serving: 1 starch, 1½ meat (1 carb)

COOK'S TIPS

- Lean (90%) ground beef, cooked and drained, can be substituted for the ground turkey, if desired.

- Cajun seasoning can be substituted for the Cajun Herb Seasoning Mix, if desired.

- This recipe looks nice on our glazed **Round Platter**, an attractive serving piece that will complement just about any table setting.

- The Grill Pan is the perfect way to get delicious grilled flavor and attractive grill marks on food without setting foot out of the house. For best results, heat the pan over medium-high heat 5 minutes before adding food.

- If desired, ½ cup prepared barbecue sauce can be substituted for the ketchup, vinegar and Barbecue Seasoning Mix.

TANGY GRILLED CHICKEN PIZZA

Prep time: 30 minutes • Cook time: 18-22 minutes • Stand time: 10 minutes

The Professional Grill Pan brings the smoky flavor of the grill indoors when you prepare the chicken to top this flavorful barbecue pizza.

2 boneless, skinless chicken breast halves (about 4 ounces each)
Salt and ground black pepper

2 packages (10 ounces each) refrigerated pizza crust

½ cup ketchup

1 teaspoon cider vinegar

1½ tablespoons **Pantry Barbecue Seasoning Mix**

1 garlic clove, pressed

1 small red onion, sliced into rings

1 can (3.25 ounces) pitted ripe olives, drained and chopped

¼ cup snipped fresh parsley

2 cups (8 ounces) shredded Colby & Monterey Jack cheese blend, divided

¼ cup (1 ounce) grated fresh Parmesan cheese

1. Preheat oven to 425°F. Season chicken on both sides with salt and black pepper; lightly spray chicken with vegetable oil using **Kitchen Spritzer**. Heat **Professional Grill Pan** over medium-high heat. Add chicken; cook 4-5 minutes on each side or until chicken is no longer pink. Remove from pan; cool 10 minutes. Dice chicken; set aside.

2. Lightly sprinkle **Large Round Stone** with flour. Unroll both packages of pizza dough and arrange side by side on baking stone, shaping into a circle. Using lightly floured **Baker's Roller**™, roll dough to edge of baking stone, pressing seams to seal. In **Small Batter Bowl**, combine ketchup, vinegar, seasoning mix and garlic pressed with **Garlic Press**; mix well. Spread barbecue sauce over crust to within ½ inch of edge.

3. Slice red onion using **Ultimate Slice & Grate**. Chop olives using **Food Chopper**. In large **Colander Bowl**, toss chicken, onion, olives, parsley and 1½ cups of the Colby-Jack cheese. Spread chicken mixture over dough to within ½ inch of edge; sprinkle with remaining Colby-Jack cheese. Grate Parmesan cheese over pizza using **Deluxe Cheese Grater**.

4. Bake 18-22 minutes or until crust is golden brown. Remove from oven; let stand 10 minutes. Cut into wedges.

Yield: 8 servings

Nutrients per serving: Calories 600, Total Fat 19 g, Saturated Fat 8 g, Cholesterol 50 mg, Carbohydrate 76 g, Protein 27 g, Sodium 1620 mg, Fiber 3 g

Diabetic exchanges per serving: 2 meat, 4 starch, 1 fruit, 1 vegetable, 1 fat (5 carb)

- Florentine means "in the style of Florence, Italy," and refers to dishes with spinach as a main ingredient.

- Even if you buy prewashed spinach, it's a good idea to thoroughly wash and drain the leaves in the large **Colander** to remove any dirt and grit.

FLORENTINE BRUNCH CASSEROLE

Prep time: 45 minutes • Bake time: 15-20 minutes

Fresh spinach and red bell peppers shine through in this creamy and colorful egg casserole, perfect for any brunch buffet.

12-16 slices firm white sandwich bread

3 tablespoons butter or margarine, divided

1 can (10¾ ounces) condensed cream of celery soup

⅓ cup milk

¼ teaspoon coarsely ground black pepper

⅓ cup finely chopped onion

1 red bell pepper, diced (about 1 cup)

4 ounces deli baked ham, diced (about ½ cup)

10 eggs, lightly beaten

1 cup (4 ounces) shredded cheddar cheese, divided

1 bag (5 ounces) fresh spinach leaves, washed and stemmed (about 6 cups)

1. Preheat oven to 375°F. Cut crusts off bread; cube crusts to measure 2 cups. Arrange bread slices in an overlapping pattern against sides of **Oval Baker**; place bread cubes in bottom of baker. Microwave 2 tablespoons of the butter in **Small Micro-Cooker®** on HIGH 30 seconds or until melted; lightly brush over bread slices. Bake 15-20 minutes or until edges of bread are golden brown.

2. Meanwhile, in **Small Batter Bowl**, whisk soup, milk and black pepper until smooth. Finely chop onion using **Food Chopper**. Dice bell pepper and ham using **Chef's Knife**. Melt remaining butter in **Family (12-in.) Skillet** over medium heat; add onion and bell pepper. Cook 5 minutes or until vegetables are tender; stir in ham. Whisk eggs in **Classic Batter Bowl**; add to skillet. Cook over medium-high heat, stirring occasionally, until eggs are set but still moist.

3. Stir in soup mixture; cook 1 minute or until hot. Grate cheese using **Deluxe Cheese Grater**. Gently stir ¾ cup of the cheese into egg mixture; fold in spinach, half at a time. Cook about 2 minutes, stirring gently until spinach is wilted.

4. Spoon egg mixture into center of baker, mounding slightly in center. Top with remaining ¼ cup cheese. Serve immediately.

Yield: 8 servings

Nutrients per serving: Calories 340, Total Fat 19 g, Saturated Fat 9 g, Cholesterol 300 mg, Carbohydrate 25 g, Protein 18 g, Sodium 810 mg, Fiber 1 g

Diabetic exchanges per serving: 2 meat, 1 vegetable, 1 starch, 1½ fat (1 carb)

PEACHY CHEESE COFFEE CAKE

Prep time: 25 minutes • Bake time: 25-30 minutes • Cool time: 15 minutes

This coffee cake is a variation of the celebrated Cherry Cheese Coffee Cake, a recipe that has been one of our favorites for years.

Coffee Cake & Filling

2 packages (8 ounces each) refrigerated crescent rolls

1 package (8 ounces) cream cheese, softened

¼ cup powdered sugar

1 egg yolk

½ teaspoon vanilla or almond extract

1 can (21 ounces) peach, cherry or apple pie filling

Glaze

½ cup powdered sugar

2-3 teaspoons milk

1. Preheat oven to 350°F. Unroll crescent dough. Separate into 16 triangles, reserving four triangles for decoration. On **Large Round Stone**, arrange 12 triangles in a circle with wide ends toward the outside edge of baking stone and points toward the center. (Points will not meet.) Using lightly floured **Baker's Roller**™, roll dough to a 14-inch circle, pressing seams together to seal. (There should be a 3-inch-diameter opening in center.) Form a slightly raised rim along inner and outer edges of dough.

2. In **Classic Batter Bowl**, combine cream cheese, powdered sugar, egg yolk and vanilla; whisk until smooth. Spread cream cheese mixture evenly over dough to within ½ inch of edge. Spoon pie filling evenly over cream cheese mixture.

3. Using **Pizza Cutter**, cut each remaining dough triangle lengthwise into three strips. Arrange dough strips evenly in spoke-like fashion over filling. Press ends to seal at center and outer edges. Bake 25-30 minutes or until golden brown. Remove from oven; cool 15 minutes.

4. For glaze, combine powdered sugar and milk; mix until smooth. Drizzle evenly over coffee cake. Cut into wedges. Serve warm.

Yield: 12 servings

Nutrients per serving: Calories 290, Total Fat 15 g, Saturated Fat 6 g, Cholesterol 40 mg, Carbohydrate 32 g, Protein 5 g, Sodium 370 mg, Fiber less than 1 g

Diabetic exchanges per serving: 2 starch, 3 fat (2 carb)

COOK'S TIPS

- To soften cream cheese, microwave on HIGH 30 seconds or until softened.

- Use the **Small Spreader** to easily spread the cream cheese mixture over the dough.

- For a lighter coffee cake, substitute reduced-fat crescent rolls and fat-free cream cheese for the crescent rolls and cream cheese.

- For an elegant touch, garnish this coffee cake with edible flowers, which can be found in the produce section of larger supermarkets, packaged with fresh herbs. Some popular edible flowers are nasturtiums and violets.

- Ground cinnamon can be substituted for the Korintje Cinnamon, if desired.

- To pipe glaze over rolls, place a small, resealable plastic food storage bag inside **Measure All®Cup**. Pour glaze into corner of bag. Twist top of bag; secure with **Twixit! Clip**. Cut a small tip off corner of bag to allow glaze to flow through. Pipe glaze over tree to form a garland.

MINI CINNAMON CHRISTMAS TREE ROLLS

Prep time: 35 minutes • Bake time: 20-25 minutes • Cool time: 15 minutes

Surprise holiday guests with these easy, festive rolls arranged in a tree-shaped pattern.

Cinnamon Rolls

½ cup *each:* red and green maraschino cherries, drained and chopped

2 packages (8 ounces each) refrigerated crescent rolls

2 tablespoons butter or margarine, softened

¼ cup granulated sugar

1 teaspoon **Pantry Korintje Cinnamon**

Glaze

¾ cup powdered sugar

2-3 teaspoons milk

Additional red and green maraschino cherries, halved (optional)

1. Preheat oven to 375°F. For cinnamon rolls, chop maraschino cherries with **Food Chopper**; set aside. Unroll one package of crescent roll dough on lightly floured surface; do not separate. Using **Baker's Roller™**, roll dough to seal perforations. Repeat with second package of dough. Do not join dough together. Spread butter evenly over dough. Combine granulated sugar and cinnamon in **Flour/Sugar Shaker**; sprinkle evenly over dough. Sprinkle chopped cherries over sugar mixture.

2. Starting at short end, roll up dough jelly roll style to make two 9-inch-long rolls. Pinch edges to seal. Cut each roll crosswise into ¾-inch slices to make 12 slices (24 rolls total).

3. Place slices, cut side down, on **Large Round Stone** to form a tree. Beginning 2 inches from edge of baking stone, place one slice for top. Arrange two slices below with sides touching. Continue arranging a row of three slices, then a row of four slices and a row of five slices. Place six slices in the bottom row. Use the remaining slices for the trunk, centering two slices under the last row, and last slice below.

4. Bake 20-25 minutes or until rolls are golden brown. Remove from oven; cool 15 minutes. For glaze, mix powdered sugar and milk until smooth; drizzle over warm rolls. Garnish with additional cherries, if desired. Serve warm.

Yield: 24 mini cinnamon rolls

Nutrients per serving (1 roll): Calories 110, Total Fat 5 g, Saturated Fat 1.5 g, Cholesterol less than 5 mg, Carbohydrate 15 g, Protein 1 g, Sodium 160 mg, Fiber 0 g

Diabetic exchanges per serving (1 roll): 1 fruit, 1 fat (1 carb)

DOUBLE CHOCOLATE SWIRL BREAD

Prep time: 20 minutes • Bake time: 25-30 minutes • Cool time: 55 minutes

Chocolate lovers, rejoice! Slice open these delicious loaves to reveal an intense swirl of chocolate and almonds.

Bread

- ½ cup sliced almonds, coarsely chopped
- ½ cup white chocolate morsels, chopped
- 2 packages (11 ounces each) refrigerated French bread dough
- 1 egg white
- 1 tablespoon water
- ¼ cup semi-sweet chocolate morsels, grated, divided

Chocolate Drizzle

- ½ cup white or semi-sweet chocolate morsels
- 1 teaspoon vegetable oil
- Additional sliced almonds or chocolate morsels (optional)

1. Preheat oven to 375°F. For bread, lightly spray **Mini Loaf Pan** with nonstick cooking spray. Coarsely chop almonds and white chocolate morsels; place in **Classic Batter Bowl**.

2. Unroll one package of the bread dough on lightly floured surface; do not stretch. Lightly beat egg white and water in **Small Batter Bowl**; brush dough with a portion of the egg white mixture. Grate half of the semi-sweet chocolate morsels evenly over dough. Sprinkle with half of the almond and white chocolate mixture; roll lightly with **Baker's Roller™**, pressing mixture into dough.

3. Unroll remaining package of bread dough directly over first dough layer, matching edges and rolling lightly to seal. Brush dough lightly with a portion of the egg white mixture. Grate remaining chocolate morsels over dough. Sprinkle with remaining white chocolate and almond mixture; roll lightly with Baker's Roller.

4. Starting at narrow edge, roll dough up tightly; pinch edge to seal. Slice roll into four equal portions; place seam side down in pan. Make deep cut down the length of each loaf without cutting through ends. Brush loaves with remaining egg white mixture. Bake 25-30 minutes or until golden brown. Remove from oven; cool in pan 5 minutes. Remove loaves from pan. Cool completely.

5. For chocolate drizzle, place chocolate morsels and oil in **Small Micro-Cooker®**; microwave, uncovered, on HIGH 30-40 seconds or until chocolate is melted and smooth. (Do not overheat.) Drizzle over loaves; sprinkle with additional almonds or chocolate morsels, if desired.

Yield: 16 servings

Nutrients per serving: Calories 190, Total Fat 7 g, Saturated Fat 3 g, Cholesterol less than 5 mg, Carbohydrate 27 g, Protein 5 g, Sodium 260 mg, Fiber 0 g

Diabetic exchanges per serving: 2 starch, 1 fat (2 carb)

Variation: *White Chocolate Cherry Swirl Bread:* Substitute ½ cup chopped maraschino cherries for the grated semi-sweet chocolate morsels; proceed as recipe directs. Drizzle finished loaves as directed in Step 5; garnish with halved maraschino cherries and sliced almonds.

Lightly brush dough with a portion of the egg white mixture. Grate half of the semi-sweet chocolate morsels over dough; sprinkle with half of the almond and white chocolate mixture.

Unroll remaining package of bread dough over first layer. Repeat as described above. Starting at narrow edge, roll dough up tightly; pinch seam to seal.

Slice roll into four equal portions; place seam side down in pan.

APRICOT ALMOND TWIST

Prep time: 20 minutes • Bake time: 30-32 minutes • Cool time: 10 minutes

This beautiful fruit-filled bread will be a welcome addition to any brunch spread.

- For how-to photos for filling and shaping the twist, see *Bistro Chicken Twist* (p. 55).

- Dried cherries or raisins can be substituted for the sweetened dried cranberries, if desired.

- The fine mesh screen of the **Flour/Sugar Shaker** allows you to evenly sprinkle flour over the surface of a cutting board or dough to prevent sticking. It is also perfect for sprinkling powdered sugar, cinnamon sugar or cocoa powder over baked goods for a pretty finishing touch.

- Brushing the dough with egg white before baking will give the finished bread a shiny, deep golden brown appearance.

- Eggs will separate more easily when cold. Use the **Egg Separator**, which conveniently attaches to the rim of most bowls, to separate the egg yolk from the egg white.

1 package (6-7 ounces) dried apricots, diced (about 1 cup)
¾ cup white chocolate morsels
½ cup sweetened dried cranberries
3 tablespoons all-purpose flour
½ teaspoon almond extract
1 tablespoon water
2 packages (11 ounces each) refrigerated French bread dough
1 egg white, lightly beaten
⅓ cup sliced almonds
  Powdered sugar (optional)

1. Preheat oven to 375°F. Dice apricots using **Chef's Knife**. Place apricots, chocolate morsels, cranberries, flour and almond extract in **Classic Batter Bowl**; mix well. Add water; mix well.

2. Place bread dough, seam sides up, on smooth side of **Large Grooved Cutting Board**. Using **Serrated Bread Knife**, slice each loaf lengthwise, end to end, cutting halfway through to center of loaf; spread open flat. Lightly sprinkle additional flour evenly over dough. Using **Baker's Roller**™, roll dough crosswise to a 4-inch width, creating a well down center of each loaf.

3. Spoon half of the apricot mixture down center of each loaf. Gather up edges over filling, pinching firmly to seal. Place loaves, seam sides down, in an "X" pattern on **Rectangle Stone**. Crisscross ends of dough to form a large figure "8," keeping ends of dough 1 inch from edge of stone and leaving two 1½-inch openings in center of twist.

4. Lightly brush egg white over dough using **Pastry Brush**. Cut a 3-inch slit in each of the top sections of the twist to reveal filling.

5. Sprinkle almonds evenly over dough, pressing gently. Bake 30-32 minutes or until deep golden brown. Remove from oven; cool 10 minutes. Sprinkle with powdered sugar, if desired. Cut into slices. Serve warm.

Yield: 16 servings

Nutrients per serving: Calories 200, Total Fat 5 g, Saturated Fat 2 g, Cholesterol 0 mg, Carbohydrate 35 g, Protein 5 g, Sodium 260 mg, Fiber 1 g

Diabetic exchanges per serving: 2 starch, 1 fat (2 carb)

CINNAMON CRUNCH COBBLESTONE MUFFINS

Prep time: 15 minutes • Bake time: 20-25 minutes

These pull-apart muffins, baked in our Stoneware Muffin Pan, can be prepared in no time for a wonderful breakfast treat or afternoon pick-me-up.

¼ cup pecan halves, chopped

⅔ cup sugar

1 tablespoon **Pantry Korintje Cinnamon**

2 packages (11.3 ounces each) refrigerated dinner rolls

⅓ cup butter or margarine, melted, divided

1 tablespoon all-purpose flour

1. Preheat oven to 375°F. Chop pecans using **Food Chopper**. Combine pecans, sugar and cinnamon in **Small Batter Bowl**; mix well.

2. Separate rolls; cut each roll into six pieces using **Pizza Cutter**. Place half of the dough pieces and 2 tablespoons of the butter in **Classic Batter Bowl**; toss gently to coat. Sprinkle with ¼ cup of the sugar mixture; toss to coat. Divide dough pieces evenly among six muffin cups in **Stoneware Muffin Pan**. Repeat with remaining dough, 2 tablespoons of the butter and ¼ cup of the sugar mixture; divide evenly to fill remaining muffin cups.

3. Add flour to remaining sugar mixture in batter bowl; add remaining butter and mix until crumbly. Using **Small Scoop**, place a scant scoop of crumb topping over each muffin.

4. Bake 20-25 minutes or until muffins are deep golden brown. Remove from oven. Cool in pan 5 minutes. Remove from pan. Serve warm.

Yield: 12 muffins

Nutrients per serving: Calories 250, Total Fat 9 g, Saturated Fat 3.5 g, Cholesterol 15 mg, Carbohydrate 36 g, Protein 6 g, Sodium 50 mg, Fiber 2 g

Diabetic exchanges per serving: 2 starch, 2 fat (2 carb)

COOK'S TIPS

- Ground cinnamon can be substituted for the Korintje Cinnamon, if desired.

- You'll find the **Small Micro-Cooker®** especially handy for melting butter and chocolate and for heating foods of all kinds. To avoid spattering, microwave the butter, covered, on HIGH 30-45 seconds or until melted.

- These muffins are best when served warm right from the oven.

Simple
SHAPES
&
Fabulous
FILLINGS

Choose a shape and fill it with one
of our eight fabulous fillings!

*Pictured from left to right: Beef Taco Ring (p. 80), Chicken &
Broccoli Wreath (p. 82), Spinach & Artichoke Braid (p. 81)*

Simple SHAPES

The Wreath, Ring and Braid have been hailed as some of our most popular recipes. Flaky pastry is filled with a savory filling for a dramatic main dish that can be prepared in less than an hour. Choose a distinctive shape, then fill it with one of the eight fabulous fillings we've included on the next few pages. It's as easy as that!

MAKING THE WREATH

Unroll 2 (8-ounce) packages refrigerated crescent rolls; separate into 16 triangles. Arrange eight triangles in a circle on **Large Round Stone** with wide ends 3 inches from edge of baking stone and points towards the outside. (Points will extend off the edge of the baking stone.) Arrange remaining triangles in center of baking stone, matching wide ends with triangles already in place. (Points will overlap in center.)

Using **Baker's Roller**™, roll over seams of triangles where wide ends meet, creating a smooth surface for filling. Do not seal center triangles.

Using **Large Scoop**, scoop filling evenly over dough in a continuous circle.

Beginning with last triangle placed in center of baking stone, bring point of triangle straight across filling. Next, bring point of opposite outside triangle diagonally across filling, covering point of previous triangle. (Filling will show.) Repeat, overlapping points of inside and outside triangles to form a wreath. Tuck last end under first. Continue as recipe directs.

MAKING THE RING

Unroll 2 (8-ounce) packages refrigerated crescent rolls; separate into 16 triangles. Arrange triangles, slightly overlapping, in a circle on **Large Round Stone** with wide ends 4 inches from edge of baking stone. (Points will extend off the edge of the baking stone.) Roll wide ends of dough toward center to create a 5-inch opening.

Using **Large Scoop**, scoop filling evenly over dough in a continuous circle.

Bring points of triangles up over filling and tuck under dough at center to form a ring. (Filling will show.) Continue as recipe directs.

MAKING THE BRAID

Unroll 2 (8-ounce) packages refrigerated crescent rolls; do not separate. Arrange dough on **Rectangle Stone** with longest sides of rectangles across width of baking stone. Roll dough to seal seams.

Starting on longest sides of baking stone, cut sides of dough into eight strips, about 1½ inches wide and 3 inches long. Using **Large Scoop**, scoop filling evenly over center of dough.

Starting at one end, lift one strip of dough; twist one turn and lay across top of filling. Repeat, alternating strips of dough to form a braid. Fold bottom edges of dough up at ends of braid. Continue as recipe directs.

CLASSIC REUBEN

8 ounces sliced deli corned beef, chopped (2 cups)

1 can (8 ounces) sauerkraut, drained and squeezed dry

1¼ cups (5 ounces) shredded Swiss cheese, divided

¼ cup Thousand Island dressing

2 tablespoons snipped fresh parsley

1 garlic clove, pressed

1 egg white, lightly beaten

1. Preheat oven to 375°F. In **Classic Batter Bowl**, combine corned beef, sauerkraut, 1 cup of the cheese, dressing, parsley and garlic; mix well.

2. Scoop filling evenly over desired shape; finish shape as directed. Brush with egg white. Sprinkle with remaining cheese. Bake 25-30 minutes or until golden brown.

Yield: 8 servings

Nutrients per serving: Calories 360, Total Fat 22 g, Saturated Fat 7 g, Cholesterol 35 mg, Carbohydrate 26 g, Protein 15 g, Sodium 1120 mg, Fiber less than 1 g

Diabetic exchanges per serving: 2 starch, 1 meat, 3 fat (2 carb)

BEEF TACO

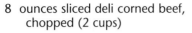

Fabulous
FILLINGS

1½ pounds lean (90%) ground beef

1 package (1-1.25 ounces) taco seasoning mix

1¾ cups (7 ounces) shredded cheddar cheese, divided

2 tablespoons water

1 egg white, lightly beaten

Optional toppings: salsa, shredded lettuce, chopped onion and tomato, sliced olives and sour cream

1. Preheat oven to 375°F. Cook ground beef in **Large (10-in.) Skillet** over medium heat 10-12 minutes or until no longer pink, breaking beef into crumbles; drain. Stir in taco seasoning mix, 1½ cups of the cheese and water.

2. Scoop filling evenly over desired shape; finish shape as directed. Brush with egg white. Sprinkle with remaining cheese. Bake 25-30 minutes or until golden brown. Serve with toppings.

Yield: 8 servings

Nutrients per serving: Calories 470, Total Fat 27 g, Saturated Fat 11 g, Cholesterol 55 mg, Carbohydrate 26 g, Protein 27 g, Sodium 980 mg, Fiber 0 g

Diabetic exchanges per serving: 2 starch, 2 meat, 2 fat (2 carb)

SPINACH & ARTICHOKE

1 can (14 ounces) artichoke hearts in water, drained and chopped

1 package (10 ounces) frozen chopped spinach, thawed and well drained

1 cup (4 ounces) shredded mozzarella cheese

1 package (4 ounces) crumbled feta cheese

1/2 cup diced red bell pepper

1/3 cup mayonnaise

1 garlic clove, pressed

1/4 teaspoon coarsely ground black pepper

1 egg white, lightly beaten

2 tablespoons (1/2 ounce) grated fresh Parmesan cheese

1. Preheat oven to 375°F. In **Classic Batter Bowl**, combine artichokes, spinach, mozzarella cheese, feta cheese, bell pepper, mayonnaise, garlic and black pepper; mix well.

2. Scoop filling evenly over desired shape; finish shape as directed. Brush with egg white. Sprinkle with grated Parmesan cheese. Bake 25-30 minutes or until golden brown.

Yield: 8 servings

Nutrients per serving: Calories 400, Total Fat 26 g, Saturated Fat 8 g, Cholesterol 25 mg, Carbohydrate 29 g, Protein 13 g, Sodium 810 mg, Fiber 3 g

Diabetic exchanges per serving: 1 meat, 2 starch, 4 fat (2 carb)

CHICKEN CLUB

3 cups coarsely chopped cooked chicken

4 slices bacon, crisply cooked, drained and chopped

1 cup (4 ounces) shredded Swiss cheese, divided

1/3 cup mayonnaise

1 teaspoon Dijon mustard

2 tablespoons snipped fresh parsley

1 garlic clove, pressed

2 plum tomatoes, sliced

1 egg white, lightly beaten

1. Preheat oven to 375°F. In **Classic Batter Bowl**, combine chicken, bacon, 3/4 cup of the cheese, mayonnaise, mustard, parsley and garlic; mix well.

2. Scoop filling evenly over desired shape; top with tomato slices. Finish shape as directed. Brush with egg white. Sprinkle with remaining cheese. Bake 25-30 minutes or until golden brown.

Yield: 8 servings

Nutrients per serving: Calories 440, Total Fat 26 g, Saturated Fat 8 g, Cholesterol 60 mg, Carbohydrate 24 g, Protein 25 g, Sodium 660 mg, Fiber less than 1 g

Diabetic exchanges per serving: 1 1/2 starch, 3 meat, 2 1/2 fat (1 1/2 carb)

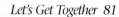

TURKEY & CRANBERRY

2 cups chopped cooked turkey

1¼ cups (5 ounces) shredded Swiss cheese

½ cup sliced celery

½ cup sweetened dried cranberries

3 tablespoons snipped fresh parsley

½ cup mayonnaise

2 tablespoons honey Dijon mustard

½ teaspoon coarsely ground black pepper

1 egg white, lightly beaten

1. Preheat oven to 375°F. In **Classic Batter Bowl**, combine turkey, 1 cup of the cheese, celery, cranberries, parsley, mayonnaise, mustard and black pepper; mix well.

2. Scoop filling evenly over desired shape; finish shape as directed. Brush with egg white. Sprinkle with remaining cheese. Bake 25-30 minutes or until golden brown.

Yield: 8 servings

Nutrients per serving: Calories 480, Total Fat 30 g, Saturated Fat 8 g, Cholesterol 50 mg, Carbohydrate 30 g, Protein 20 g, Sodium 700 mg, Fiber less than 1 g

Diabetic exchanges per serving: 2 starch, 4 meat, 4 fat (2 carb)

Fabulous FILLINGS

CHICKEN & BROCCOLI

2 cups coarsely chopped cooked chicken

1½ cups coarsely chopped broccoli

1 cup (4 ounces) shredded cheddar cheese

½ cup diced red bell pepper

⅓ cup mayonnaise

2 teaspoons **Pantry All-Purpose Dill Mix** or dried dill weed

¼ teaspoon salt

1 garlic clove, pressed

1 egg white, lightly beaten

¼ cup slivered almonds

1. Preheat oven to 375°F. In **Classic Batter Bowl**, combine chicken, broccoli, cheese, bell pepper, mayonnaise, seasoning mix, salt and garlic; mix well.

2. Scoop filling over desired shape; finish shape as directed. Brush with egg white. Sprinkle with almonds. Bake 25-30 minutes or until golden brown.

Yield: 8 servings

Nutrients per serving: Calories 440, Total Fat 29 g, Saturated Fat 8 g, Cholesterol 50 mg, Carbohydrate 25 g, Protein 19 g, Sodium 700 mg, Fiber less than 1 g

Diabetic exchanges per serving: 1 starch, 2½ meat, 3 fat, 2 vegetable (1 carb)

BARBECUE CHICKEN

2 cups chopped cooked chicken

2 cups (8 ounces) shredded Monterey Jack cheese blend, divided

1 can (3.25 ounces) pitted ripe olives, sliced

½ cup thinly sliced green onions with tops

½ cup chili sauce

2 tablespoons **Pantry Barbecue Seasoning Mix**

1 garlic clove, pressed

1 egg white, lightly beaten

1. Preheat oven to 375°F. In **Classic Batter Bowl**, combine chicken, 1¾ cups of the cheese, olives, green onions, chili sauce, seasoning mix and garlic; mix well.

2. Scoop filling evenly over desired shape; finish shape as directed. Brush with egg white. Sprinkle with remaining cheese. Bake 25-30 minutes or golden brown.

Yield: 8 servings

Nutrients per serving: Calories 410, Total Fat 22 g, Saturated Fat 9 g, Cholesterol 40 mg, Carbohydrate 32 g, Protein 18 g, Sodium 1090 mg, Fiber 0 g

Diabetic exchanges per serving: 2 starch, 2 meat, 2 fat (2 carb)

GARDEN VEGETABLE OMELET

4 ounces cream cheese, softened

¼ cup milk

1 tablespoon all-purpose flour

8 eggs, divided

1 teaspoon **Pantry All-Purpose Dill Mix**

¼ teaspoon salt

¼ pound fresh asparagus spears, cut into 1-inch pieces (¾ cup) *brocoli*

½ cup diced red bell pepper *green*

⅓ cup chopped onion *(red onion) chop big pieces*

1 tablespoon butter or margarine

½ cup (2 ounces) shredded cheddar cheese

1 c. ham cubes
3 or 4 slices ½" thick

1. Preheat oven to 375°F. In **Classic Batter Bowl**, whisk cream cheese and milk; add flour and whisk until smooth. Separate 1 egg; reserve egg white. Add the yolk, remaining 7 eggs, dill mix, salt and black pepper to cream cheese mixture; whisk until smooth. Add asparagus, bell pepper and onion to batter bowl; mix well.

2. Melt butter in **Family (12-in.) Skillet** over medium heat. Add egg mixture; cook, stirring occasionally, 4-6 minutes until eggs are set but still moist. Remove pan from heat. Scoop filling evenly over desired shape; sprinkle with cheese. Finish shape as directed. Brush with remaining lightly beaten egg white. Bake 25-30 minutes or until golden brown. *then add ham.*

Yield: 8 servings

Nutrients per serving: Calories 320, Total Fat 21 g, Saturated Fat 9 g, Cholesterol 25 mg, Carbohydrate 26 g, Protein 7 g, Sodium 620 mg, Fiber 0 g

Diabetic exchanges per serving: 1 meat, 2 fruit, 3 fat (2 carb)

Save
Room for
DESSERT

From simple treats
to dazzling sweets.

Cherry Almond Angel Roll (p. 86)

Pour batter over Parchment Paper, spreading evenly; sprinkle with almonds.

Starting at short end of cake, roll up cake in Parchment Paper.

Using **Large Spreader,** spread filling over cake to within 1 inch of edges of cake.

CHERRY ALMOND ANGEL ROLL

Prep time: 30 minutes • Bake time: 30-35 minutes
Cool time: 2 hours • Chill time: 30 minutes

This delightful cake, filled with cherry preserves and almond-flavored cream, can be made well in advance. (Pictured on p. 84-85)

1 package (16 ounces) angel food cake mix
1 package (2.25 ounces) sliced almonds, chopped
½ cup powdered sugar
½ cup cherry preserves
1 container (8 ounces) sour cream
1 container (8 ounces) frozen whipped topping, thawed
½ teaspoon almond extract
2-4 drops red food coloring (optional)
1 package (3.4 ounces) white chocolate instant pudding and pie filling
Additional powdered sugar (optional)

1. Preheat oven to 350°F. Line **Stoneware Bar Pan** with a 13-inch piece of **Parchment Paper**. Prepare cake mix according to package directions. Pour batter over Parchment Paper, spreading evenly. Chop almonds using **Food Chopper**; sprinkle evenly over batter. Bake 30-35 minutes or until top springs back when lightly touched with fingertip. Remove from oven.

2. Sprinkle powdered sugar over cake using **Flour/Sugar Shaker**. Place an additional 18-inch piece of Parchment Paper over cake. Invert **Stackable Cooling Rack** over paper. Carefully invert cake; remove pan. Peel Parchment Paper from bottom side of cake; discard. Starting at short end of cake, roll up cake in Parchment Paper jelly roll style. Cool completely.

3. Unroll cake and place on smooth side of **Large Grooved Cutting Board**. Spread cake with preserves. In **Classic Batter Bowl**, combine sour cream, whipped topping, almond extract and food coloring, if desired; mix well. Add pudding mix and whisk until thickened. Spread filling over cake to within 1 inch of edge; roll up cake. Refrigerate at least 30 minutes. Sprinkle cake with additional powdered sugar, if desired. Slice using **Serrated Bread Knife**.

Yield: 12 servings

Nutrients per serving: Calories 350, Total Fat 10 g, Saturated Fat 5 g, Cholesterol 15 mg, Carbohydrate 57 g, Protein 5 g, Sodium 460 mg, Fiber less than 1 g

Diabetic exchanges per serving: 2 starch, 2 fruit, 1½ fat (4 carb)

PECAN TASSIES

Prep time: 30 minutes • Bake time: 20-25 minutes

A chewy pecan mixture fills buttery pastry cups for an all-time favorite Southern treat.
(Pictured on p. 88)

Tart Shells

½ cup butter or margarine, softened

3 ounces cream cheese, softened

1 cup all-purpose flour

Filling

2 tablespoons butter or margarine, melted

¾ cup packed brown sugar

1 egg

1 teaspoon vanilla

1 cup pecan halves, finely chopped

   Powdered sugar (optional)

1. Preheat oven to 350°F. For tart shells, beat butter and cream cheese in **Classic Batter Bowl** until well blended. Add flour; mix until a soft dough forms.

2. Using **Small Scoop**, shape dough into 1-inch balls. Place balls of dough into ungreased cups of **Deluxe Mini-Muffin Pan**. Dip **Mini-Tart Shaper** in flour; press into dough with even pressure until dough rises slightly above rim of pan.

3. For filling, place butter in **Small Batter Bowl**; microwave on HIGH 30 seconds or until melted. Stir in brown sugar, egg and vanilla. Finely chop pecans using **Food Chopper**; add to batter bowl and mix well.

4. Using Small Scoop, fill each tart shell with level scoop of filling (do not overfill). Bake 20-25 minutes or until edges are light golden brown. Remove from oven, cool in pan 3 minutes. Remove from pan to **Stackable Cooling Rack**; cool completely. Sprinkle with powdered sugar, if desired.

Yield: 24 tarts

Nutrients per serving (1 tart): Calories 130, Total Fat 10 g, Saturated Fat 4 g, Cholesterol 25 mg, Carbohydrate 11 g, Protein 2 g, Sodium 65 mg, Fiber less than 1 g

Diabetic exchanges per serving (1 tart): 1 starch, 1½ fat (1 carb)

- Butter will provide the best flavor when making these rich, miniature tarts.

- You'll want to be sure to lightly flour the Mini-Tart Shaper before forming each shell to prevent the dough from sticking.

- The **Flour/Sugar Shaker** is ideal for sprinkling powdered sugar over baked goods for a pretty finishing touch.

- To store tarts, cool completely, then place in a tightly covered container. For longer storage, freeze up to 1 month. To thaw, let the tarts stand at room temperature. You may want to sprinkle the tarts with additional powdered sugar before serving.

RASPBERRIES & CREAM STREUSEL SQUARES

Prep time: 20 minutes • Bake time: 30-35 minutes

These elegant-looking shortbread cookies take no time to prepare with professional-looking results.

Crust

¾ cup (1½ sticks) butter or margarine, melted

2½ cups all-purpose flour

¾ cup powdered sugar

Filling

1 jar (12 ounces) seedless raspberry or apricot jam

¼ cup all-purpose flour

Topping

1 package (8 ounces) cream cheese, softened

½ cup powdered sugar

¼ cup walnut halves, chopped

1. Preheat oven to 350°F. For crust, place butter in **Classic Batter Bowl**; microwave on HIGH 1 minute or until melted. Add flour and powdered sugar; mix until crumbly. Reserve ¼ cup of the crust mixture for topping. Sprinkle remaining crust mixture evenly over bottom of **Stoneware Bar Pan**; roll to an even thickness using lightly floured **Baker's Roller.**™

2. For filling, combine jam and flour in **Small Batter Bowl**; mix until smooth. Spread jam mixture evenly over crust.

3. For topping, place cream cheese in **Small Micro-Cooker®**. Microwave on HIGH 30 seconds or until softened. Add powdered sugar; whisk until smooth. Attach open star tip to **Easy Accent® Decorator**; fill with cream cheese mixture. Pipe cream cheese mixture in diagonal rows, 1½ inches apart, onto jam layer. Chop walnuts using **Food Chopper**. Combine nuts and reserved crust mixture; sprinkle evenly over topping.

4. Bake 30-35 minutes or until edges are light golden brown. Remove from oven; cool completely. Cut into squares.

Yield: 32 squares

Nutrients per serving (1 square): Calories 150, Total Fat 7 g, Saturated Fat 4.5 g, Cholesterol 20 mg, Carbohydrate 20 g, Protein 2 g, Sodium 65 mg, Fiber 0 g

Diabetic exchanges per serving (1 square): 1½ starch, 1 fruit, 1 fat (1½ carb)

COOK'S TIPS

- Use the **Large Spreader** for spreading the jam in an even layer over the crust.

- For variety, prepare two flavors of streusel squares at once. Combine ½ cup of raspberry jam with 2 tablespoons of flour; spread over half of the prepared crust. Combine ½ cup of apricot jam with 2 tablespoons of flour; spread over the remaining half of the crust. Proceed as directed in Steps 3 and 4.

- This recipe can be prepared in the **Square (9-in.) Baker**, if desired. Divide all ingredients in half. Proceed as recipe directs. Cut into 16 squares.

Pecan Tassies (p. 87),
Raspberries & Cream Streusel Squares

LEMON BLUEBERRY TRIFLE

Prep time: 20 minutes • Chill time: 30 minutes

What could be simpler than a trifle? This version features fresh blueberries, a creamy lemon pudding and prepared pound cake for a fast and fabulous dessert.

1 frozen prepared pound cake
    (16 ounces)
2 lemons
1½ cups milk
1 container (8 ounces) sour cream
1 container (8 ounces) frozen whipped
    topping, thawed, divided
2 packages (3.4 ounces each) lemon
    instant pudding and pie filling
1 pint blueberries
1 square (1 ounce) white chocolate for
    baking

1. Cut pound cake into 1-inch cubes; place in large **Colander Bowl**. Zest one lemon using **Lemon Zester/Scorer**; set aside. Juice same lemon using **Juicer**. Sprinkle lemon juice over pound cake cubes; toss gently.

2. In **Classic Batter Bowl**, combine milk, sour cream, half of the whipped topping and reserved lemon zest; whisk until smooth. Add pudding mix; whisk until mixture begins to thicken.

3. Set aside 10 blueberries for garnish. To assemble trifle, place one-third of the cake cubes into bottom of 10-cup serving bowl. Top with one-third of the blueberries. Using **Deluxe Cheese Grater**, grate one-fourth of the chocolate over blueberries. Top with one-third of the pudding mixture, spreading evenly. Repeat layers two more times. Reserve remaining chocolate for garnish.

4. Attach open star tip to **Easy Accent®️ Decorator**; fill with remaining whipped topping. Pipe 10 rosettes around edge of serving bowl. Score remaining lemon lengthwise using Lemon Zester/Scorer; slice lemon into five ¼-inch slices. Cut each slice in half and place between rosettes. Place one reserved blueberry on each rosette. Grate remaining chocolate in center. Refrigerate at least 30 minutes before serving.

Yield: 10 servings

Nutrients per serving: Calories 340, Total Fat 14 g, Saturated Fat 10 g, Cholesterol 70 mg, Carbohydrate 46 g, Protein 4 g, Sodium 380 mg, Fiber 1 g

Diabetic exchanges per serving: 1 starch, 2 fruit, 3 fat (3 carb)

COOK'S TIPS

- It's not necessary to thaw the pound cake. It will be easier to cut into cubes using the **Serrated Bread Knife** if it is left frozen.

- This trifle is a great make-ahead recipe. It can be assembled several hours before serving, or even the night before.

TAFFY APPLE PIZZA

Prep time: 25 minutes • Bake time: 16-18 minutes • Cool time: 1 hour

*Sliced apples, caramel topping and crunchy peanuts top a giant
sugar cookie for this Pampered Chef® classic.*

- The **Large Spreader**
  is handy for
  spreading the cream
  cheese mixture over
  the cooled cookie.
  Our **Small Spreader**
  works equally well
  for spreading frosting
  and thick glazes over
  baked goods.

- Dip apple slices in
  lemon-lime flavored
  carbonated soda or
  lemon juice to
  prevent them from
  turning brown.

- Add a touch of spice
  to this dessert pizza
  by sprinkling ground
  cinnamon over the
  apple slices in
  Step 3 using the
  Flour/Sugar Shaker.

1 package (18 ounces) refrigerated
  sugar cookie dough
1 package (8 ounces) cream cheese,
  softened
½ cup packed brown sugar
¼ cup creamy peanut butter
½ teaspoon vanilla
2 medium Granny Smith apples
¼ cup caramel ice cream topping
½ cup peanuts, chopped

1. Preheat oven to 350°F. Shape cookie
   dough into a ball and place in center of
   Large Round Stone; flatten slightly.
   Using lightly floured **Baker's Roller**™, roll
   dough to a 14-inch circle, about ¼ inch
   thick. Bake 16-18 minutes or until light
   golden brown. Remove from oven; cool
   10 minutes. Carefully loosen cookie from
   baking stone using **Serrated Bread Knife**;
   cool completely on baking stone.

2. Combine cream cheese, brown sugar,
   peanut butter and vanilla in **Small Batter
   Bowl**; mix well. Spread cream cheese
   mixture evenly over cookie.

3. Peel, core and slice apples using **Apple
   Peeler/Corer/Slicer**. Cut apple slices in
   half and arrange evenly over cream cheese
   mixture.

4. Microwave ice cream topping on HIGH
   30-45 seconds or until warm; drizzle
   evenly over apples. Chop peanuts using
   Food Chopper; sprinkle over apples. Cut
   into wedges.

Yield: 16 servings

Nutrients per serving: Calories 300, Total Fat 17 g,
Saturated Fat 5 g, Cholesterol 25 mg, Carbohydrate 36 g,
Protein 5 g, Sodium 270 mg, Fiber 1 g

Diabetic exchanges per serving: 2 starch, ½ fruit, 3 fat
(2½ carb)

PEANUT BUTTER & JELLY PIE

Prep time: 30 minutes • Bake time: 10-12 minutes
Cool time: 30 minutes • Chill time: 1 hour

This whimsical pie will remind you of your favorite childhood sandwich. It's fun for kids and grown-ups alike!

½ package (15 ounces) refrigerated pie crusts (1 crust)

¼ cup chopped peanuts, divided

1 quart strawberries (about 1 pound), divided

1 package (8 ounces) cream cheese, softened

¼ cup peanut butter

⅓ cup milk

1 container (8 ounces) frozen whipped topping, thawed, divided

1 package (3.3 ounces) white chocolate instant pudding and pie filling

¼ cup seedless strawberry jam

1. Preheat oven to 425°F. Let pie crust stand at room temperature 15 minutes. Gently unfold crust onto lightly floured surface. Roll to an 11½-inch circle using lightly floured **Baker's Roller**.™ Place crust in **Deep Dish Pie Plate**, pressing dough into bottom and up sides. Prick bottom and sides using pastry tool. Chop peanuts using **Food Chopper**; sprinkle half of the peanuts over bottom of pie crust. Bake 10-12 minutes or until light golden brown. Remove from oven; cool completely.

2. Rinse strawberries and pat dry with paper towels. Select six uniformly sized strawberries; set aside for garnish. Hull and slice remaining strawberries and arrange over bottom of crust.

3. In **Classic Batter Bowl**, combine cream cheese and peanut butter; whisk until smooth. Gradually add milk, whisking until smooth. Add half of the whipped topping and all of the pudding mix; mix until smooth using **Small Mix 'N Scraper**®. Immediately spoon filling into crust, spreading evenly.

4. Whisk jam until smooth; pour over center of filling. Spread jam into a 6-inch circle using **Small Spreader**. Attach open star tip to **Easy Accent**® **Decorator**; fill with remaining whipped topping. Pipe rosettes around edge of pie. Sprinkle remaining peanuts over pie. Slice reserved strawberries in half; arrange over whipped topping. Refrigerate at least 1 hour.

Yield: 12 servings

Nutrients per serving: Calories 310, Total Fat 19 g, Saturated Fat 9 g, Cholesterol 25 mg, Carbohydrate 29 g, Protein 4 g, Sodium 280 mg, Fiber 2 g

Diabetic exchanges per serving: 1 starch, 1 fruit, 3½ fat (2 carb)

COOK'S TIPS

■ When placing the pie crust in the Deep Dish Pie Plate, evenly ruffle the edge of the crust inside the pie plate for picture-perfect results. To keep the crust from slipping down the sides of the pie plate, firmly press the edge of the crust against the pie plate in several places.

■ The **Cook's Corer**™ and **Egg Slicer Plus**® team up in this recipe when you need to hull and slice the strawberries.

■ To soften cream cheese, microwave on HIGH 30 seconds.

■ The Small Mix 'N Scraper is a handy tool you will reach for again and again. Its heavy-duty curved head is ideal for folding thick batters and can withstand temperatures up to 650°F without melting or peeling.

■ To easily slice this cream pie, dip the **Utility Knife** in hot water before cutting it into servings.

COOL & CREAMY CHOCOLATE FONDUE

Prep time: 10 minutes • Chill time: 30 minutes

This silky, rich dessert is a decadent match for Chocolate-Drizzled Cinnamon Chips, fresh fruit and our Simple Additions™ serving pieces.

¾ cup semi-sweet chocolate morsels

1 container (8 ounces) frozen whipped topping, thawed

½ teaspoon **Pantry Korintje Cinnamon**

½ teaspoon rum or vanilla extract (optional)

Assorted fresh fruit dippers such as whole strawberries, apple, peach or pear wedges (optional)

Chocolate-Drizzled Cinnamon Chips (p. 19, optional)

1. Place chocolate morsels and half of the whipped topping in **Small Batter Bowl**. Microwave, uncovered, on HIGH 1 minute or until chocolate is melted and smooth, stirring after each 20-second interval. Fold in remaining whipped topping, cinnamon and rum extract, if desired; mix until smooth. Cover; refrigerate at least 30 minutes.

2. To serve, spoon fondue into small bowl. Serve with fruit dippers and *Chocolate-Drizzled Cinnamon Chips*, if desired.

Yield: 2 cups (16 servings)

Nutrients per serving (2 tablespoons fondue): Calories 80, Total Fat 5 g, Saturated Fat 3 g, Cholesterol 0 mg, Carbohydrate 7 g, Protein 0 g, Sodium 0 mg, Fiber 0 g

Diabetic exchanges per serving (2 tablespoons fondue): ½ fruit, 1 fat (½ carb)

Cool & Creamy Chocolate Fondue, Chocolate-Drizzled Cinnamon Chips (p. 19)

Mom's Apple Crisp

Prep time: 25 minutes • Microwave time: 14-16 minutes

This delicious dessert was developed especially for the microwave oven.
The topping becomes crisp while the fruit is delicate and tender.

6   Granny Smith apples (about 8 cups slices)
8   graham crackers (2½ x 5 inches), coarsely chopped
¾   cup packed brown sugar
½   cup all-purpose flour
½   cup quick or old-fashioned oats
1   teaspoon **Pantry Korintje Cinnamon**
½   cup butter or margarine, melted
    Vanilla ice cream (optional)

1. Peel, core and slice apples using **Apple Peeler/Corer/Slicer**. Cut apples in half; place in **Deep Dish Baker**.

2. Coarsely chop graham crackers using **Food Chopper**; place in **Classic Batter Bowl**. Add brown sugar, flour, oats and cinnamon; mix well. Place butter in **Small Micro-Cooker®**; microwave on HIGH 1 minute or until melted. Add butter to dry ingredients; mix well.

3. Sprinkle crumb mixture evenly over apples. Microwave on HIGH 14-16 minutes or until apples are tender. Cool slightly. Serve warm topped with ice cream, if desired.

Yield: 10 servings

Nutrients per serving: Calories 280, Total Fat 10 g, Saturated Fat 6 g, Cholesterol 25 mg, Carbohydrate 48 g, Protein 2 g, Sodium 140 mg, Fiber 4 g

Diabetic exchanges per serving: 1 starch, 2 fruit, 2 fat (3 carb)

COOK'S TIPS

- You'll need about 3 pounds of apples to make this recipe.

- Ground cinnamon can be substituted for the Korintje Cinnamon, if desired.

- If using a microwave oven without a built-in turntable, rotate the baker after 8 minutes of cooking.

- To prepare the crisp in a conventional oven, preheat oven to 350°F. Prepare recipe as directed. Cover loosely with aluminum foil. Bake 45 minutes; uncover and bake an additional 5-10 minutes or until apples are tender.

BANANA CREAM SUPREME

Prep time: 25 minutes • Chill time: 30 minutes

This dreamy banana dessert sets up quickly so you can savor it shortly after preparation.

- The **Baker's Roller**™ is handy for crushing graham crackers and cookies into fine crumbs for dessert crusts. Use the small roller to evenly press the crumb mixture onto the bottom of the pan.

- Create a pretty strawberry fan for garnish using the Egg Slicer Plus. Open the slicer and place the strawberry stem end down; slice most of the way through it with wires. Remove the strawberry from the wires and gently fan out the slices.

- It's best to prepare this dessert on the same day you plan to serve it so the bananas do not turn brown.

16 (2½-inch) graham cracker squares (approximately 1¼ cups crushed)
¼ cup butter or margarine, melted
3 tablespoons sugar
1 container (12 ounces) frozen whipped topping, thawed
1 container (8 ounces) sour cream
1 package (3.4 ounces) vanilla instant pudding and pie filling
3 medium bananas, sliced
2 tablespoons pecan halves, grated
   Strawberry fans (optional)

1. Finely crush graham crackers in large resealable plastic food storage bag; place in **Small Batter Bowl**. Add butter and sugar; mix well. Press crumb mixture onto bottom of **Springform Pan**.

2. In **Classic Batter Bowl**, whisk whipped topping and sour cream until blended. Add pudding mix; whisk until mixture is well blended and smooth. Spread half of the filling over crust. Slice bananas using **Egg Slicer Plus**®; arrange over filling. Spread remaining filling over bananas.

3. Grate pecans over top using **Deluxe Cheese Grater**. Refrigerate at least 30 minutes.

4. Run **Quikut Paring Knife** around sides of dessert; release collar from pan and carefully remove. Cut into wedges. Garnish each serving with a strawberry fan, if desired.

Yield: 12 servings

Nutrients per serving: Calories 270, Total Fat 14 g, Saturated Fat 10 g, Cholesterol 25 mg, Carbohydrate 32 g, Protein 2 g, Sodium 220 mg, Fiber less than 1 g

Diabetic exchanges per serving: 1 starch, 1 fruit, 3 fat (2 carb)

Variation: *Light Banana Cream Supreme:* Substitute fat-free frozen whipped topping and fat-free sour cream for the frozen whipped topping and sour cream.

Nutrients per serving: Calories 220, Total Fat 6 g, Saturated Fat 3 g, Cholesterol 10 mg, Carbohydrate 38 g, Protein 2 g, Sodium 250 mg, Fiber less than 1 g

Diabetic exchanges per serving: 1 starch, 1½ fruit, 1 fat (2½ carb)

CHOCOLATE MACAROON PIZZA

Prep time: 20 minutes • Bake time: 35-43 minutes

*This super-rich brownie pizza is reminiscent of a popular
chocolate-covered coconut candy bar.*

1 package (19-21 ounces) fudge
  brownie mix (plus ingredients to
  make brownies)

2 egg whites

1 package (14 ounces) sweetened
  flaked coconut

1 can (14 ounces) sweetened
  condensed milk (not evaporated
  milk)

1 package (2.25 ounces) sliced
  almonds

2 tablespoons (1 ounce) semi-sweet
  chocolate morsels, melted

1 teaspoon vegetable oil

1. Preheat oven to 375°F. Place a 15-inch
   circle of **Parchment Paper** on **Large
   Round Stone**. Prepare brownie mix
   according to package directions in **Classic
   Batter Bowl**. Pour brownie batter on
   Parchment Paper, spreading into a
   14-inch circle using **Large Spreader**.
   (Do not bake without Parchment Paper
   or batter will run off baking stone while
   baking.) Bake 15-18 minutes or until
   brownie is set. Do not overbake. Remove
   from oven to **Stackable Cooling Rack**.

2. In clean batter bowl, combine egg whites,
   coconut and sweetened condensed milk;
   mix well. Spread coconut mixture over
   top of brownie to within ¼ inch of edge.
   Sprinkle with almonds. Return to oven
   and bake 20-25 minutes or until edges of
   coconut are deep golden brown. Remove
   from oven to cooling rack.

3. Place chocolate morsels and oil in **Small
   Micro-Cooker®**; microwave, uncovered,
   on HIGH 45 seconds or until chocolate is
   melted and smooth, stirring after each
   10-second interval. Do not overheat.
   Drizzle chocolate over pizza. Cut into
   wedges. Serve slightly warm or at room
   temperature.

Yield: 16 servings

Nutrients per serving: Calories 450, Total Fat 22 g,
Saturated Fat 10 g, Cholesterol 35 mg, Carbohydrate 57 g,
Protein 5 g, Sodium 230 mg, Fiber 2 g

Diabetic exchanges per serving: 2 starch, 2 fruit, 4 fat (4 carb)

COOK'S TIPS

■ Be sure to choose
sweetened condensed
milk, not evaporated
milk, for this recipe.
Sweetened condensed
milk is a mixture of
whole milk and
sugar, which is heated
to produce a very
sticky, sweet mixture.
It is typically used in
baked goods, candies
and pie fillings.

■ The brownie base
can be baked earlier
in the day and
cooled. To finish the
pizza, prepare recipe
as directed in Steps
2 and 3.

■ If desired, 1 square
(1 ounce) semi-sweet
chocolate for baking
can be substituted
for the semi-sweet
chocolate morsels.

- Brushing the unbaked pie crust with egg white will help prevent it from getting soggy. Separate the egg over a small bowl using the **Egg Separator**, then whisk the egg white until light and frothy.

- Ground cinnamon can be substituted for the Korintje Cinnamon, if desired.

- You will need to purchase about 2 pounds of apples for this recipe. Any firm, red baking apples, such as Jonathan, Rome or Braeburn, can be used.

SPEEDY STREUSEL APPLE PIE

Prep time: 35 minutes • Microwave and bake time: 26-30 minutes • Stand time: 20 minutes

Give your pie a jump-start in the microwave oven, then finish baking in the conventional oven. This dual cooking method can be used for all your homemade fruit pies.

1   package (15 ounces) refrigerated pie crusts (2 crusts), divided

1   egg white, lightly beaten

¼   cup pecan halves, chopped

¾   cup plus 2 tablespoons granulated sugar, divided

1¼   teaspoons **Pantry Korintje Cinnamon**, divided

5-6   medium red baking apples, such as Jonathan (about 6 cups slices)

2   teaspoons lemon juice

1   teaspoon vanilla

3   tablespoons cornstarch

     Powdered sugar (optional)

1. Preheat oven to 400°F. Let pie crusts stand at room temperature 15 minutes. Gently unfold one pie crust onto lightly floured surface. Roll to an 11½-inch circle using lightly floured **Baker's Roller™**; place in **Deep Dish Pie Plate**, gently pressing dough into bottom and up sides. Brush egg white over bottom and halfway up sides of crust.

2. For streusel, dice remaining pie crust using **Chef's Knife** (it is not necessary to unfold crust); place in **Classic Batter Bowl**. Chop pecans using **Food Chopper**. Add pecans, 2 tablespoons of the granulated sugar and ¼ teaspoon of the cinnamon to batter bowl; toss and set aside.

3. Core and slice apples, leaving peels on, using **Apple Peeler/Corer/Slicer**; cut apple slices into quarters. In large **Colander Bowl**, combine apples, lemon juice and vanilla; toss to coat. In **Small Batter Bowl**, combine cornstarch, remaining ¾ cup granulated sugar and remaining 1 teaspoon cinnamon; mix well. Add sugar mixture to apples, stirring to coat evenly. Spoon apple mixture into crust; sprinkle evenly with reserved streusel.

4. Microwave on HIGH 8 minutes or until apples are very hot, rotating dish after 4 minutes. Remove pie from microwave; immediately place on bottom rack of conventional oven. Bake 18-22 minutes or until topping is deep golden brown. Remove from oven; let stand at least 20 minutes. Sprinkle with powdered sugar, if desired; serve warm.

Yield: 8 servings

Nutrients per serving: Calories 410, Total Fat 17 g, Saturated Fat 6 g, Cholesterol 10 mg, Carbohydrate 64 g, Protein 3 g, Sodium 200 mg, Fiber 3 g

Diabetic exchanges per serving: 1 starch, 3 fruit, 3 fat (4 carb)

AMERICAN DREAM TORTE

Prep time: 30 minutes • Bake time: 15-18 minutes
Cool time: 30 minutes • Chill time: 1 hour

Let your patriotic spirit shine with this dazzling, berry-studded cake.

1 package (16 ounces) pound cake mix
   (plus ingredients to make cake)

½ cup water

1 package (3 ounces) raspberry gelatin

¼ cup seedless raspberry jam

1 package (8 ounces) cream cheese,
   softened

⅓ cup cold milk

1 container (12 ounces) frozen
   whipped topping, thawed

1 package (3.3 ounces) white
   chocolate instant pudding and pie
   filling

¾ cup blueberries

½ cup raspberries

Fresh mint leaves (optional)

1. Preheat oven to 400°F. Line **Stoneware Bar Pan** with a 13-inch piece of **Parchment Paper**. Prepare cake mix according to package directions; pour batter into pan, spreading evenly. Bake 15-18 minutes or until **Cake Tester** inserted in center comes out clean. Remove from oven; cool 10 minutes. Lift cake onto **Stackable Cooling Rack**; cool completely.

2. In **Small Micro-Cooker®**, microwave water on HIGH 1-2 minutes or until boiling. Add gelatin; stir until dissolved. Add jam; whisk until smooth. Invert cake onto smooth side of **Large Grooved Cutting Board**; remove Parchment Paper. Prick cake at ½-inch intervals. Using **Pastry Brush**, brush cake evenly with gelatin mixture. Trim ¼ inch around edge of cake; discard edges. Cut cake crosswise into three equal layers.

3. In **Classic Batter Bowl**, whisk cream cheese and milk until smooth. Spoon whipped topping over cream cheese mixture. (Do not mix.) Sprinkle with pudding mix; mix well. (Mixture will be very thick.)

4. Place one cake layer on serving platter. Attach open star tip to **Easy Accent® Decorator**; fill with filling mixture. Pipe a straight border around edge of cake layer. Using **Large Scoop**, place four scoops of filling down center; spread evenly to border. Top with second cake layer. Repeat filling as above. For third layer, pipe a decorative border around edge. Spread remaining filling down center. Top with blueberries and raspberries. Garnish with mint leaves, if desired. Refrigerate at least 1 hour.

Yield: 16 servings

Nutrients per serving: Calories 310, Total Fat 14 g, Saturated Fat 7 g, Cholesterol 45 mg, Carbohydrate 41 g, Protein 4 g, Sodium 260 mg, Fiber 0 g

Diabetic exchanges per serving: 1 starch, 2 fruit, 2½ fat (3 carb)

MAKING THE TORTE

Using Pastry Brush, brush cake evenly with gelatin mixture.

Pipe filling around edge of one cake layer. Place four scoops of filling down center and spread evenly. Repeat with second layer.

Pipe border around edge of third cake layer. Spread remaining filling down center.

TURTLE FUDGE SKILLET CAKE

Prep time: 20 minutes • Bake time: 30-35 minutes

Baked right in our Family Skillet, this warm cake is spread with a rich caramel fudge glaze and topped with crunchy chopped pecans.

1 package (18.25 ounces) devil's food cake mix (plus ingredients to make cake)

1 tablespoon butter or margarine

4 squares (1 ounce each) semi-sweet chocolate for baking, coarsely chopped

1 jar (12 ounces) caramel ice cream topping, divided

½ cup pecan halves, coarsely chopped

Vanilla ice cream (optional)

1. Preheat oven to 350°F. Prepare cake mix according to package directions in **Classic Batter Bowl**, mixing batter by hand until smooth. Melt butter in **Family (12-in.) Skillet** over medium heat, tilting skillet to coat bottom. Gently pour batter over bottom of skillet, spreading evenly.

2. Bake, uncovered, 30-35 minutes or until **Cake Tester** inserted in center comes out clean. Using **Oven Mitts**, carefully remove skillet to **Stackable Cooling Rack**. Loosen edges of cake; carefully invert cake onto large, heat-safe serving plate.

3. Coarsely chop chocolate squares into small pieces. Place chocolate and half of the ice cream topping in **Small Micro-Cooker®**. Microwave, uncovered, on HIGH 30-60 seconds or until chocolate is melted and mixture is smooth. Carefully spread caramel and chocolate mixture over cake using **Large Spreader**.

4. Coarsely chop pecans using **Food Chopper**; sprinkle evenly over cake. Drizzle with remaining ice cream topping, if desired. Let stand until topping is set. Cut into wedges. Serve with vanilla ice cream, if desired.

Yield: 12 servings

Nutrients per serving: Calories 440, Total Fat 24 g, Saturated Fat 6 g, Cholesterol 85 mg, Carbohydrate 54 g, Protein 6 g, Sodium 490 mg, Fiber 2 g

Diabetic exchanges per serving: 2 starch, 1½ fruit, 4 fat (3½ carb)

CRISSCROSS APPLE CROWNS

Prep time: 25 minutes • Bake time: 25-30 minutes

*These treats are delicious any time of day. Serve warm with a scoop
of ice cream for a great home-style dessert.*

4 small Granny Smith apples

½ cup walnut halves, chopped

½ cup raisins

3 tablespoons all-purpose flour

¾ cup sugar, divided

1 tablespoon ground cinnamon,
   divided

1 package (17.3 ounces) grand-size flaky
   or buttermilk biscuits (8 biscuits)

1 package (10.2 ounces) grand-size flaky
   or buttermilk biscuits (5 biscuits)

1 tablespoon butter or margarine,
   melted

   Ice cream (optional)

1. Preheat oven to 350°F. Peel, core and slice
   apples using **Apple Peeler/Corer/Slicer**;
   cut apple slices into wedges using **Apple
   Wedger**. Chop walnuts using **Food
   Chopper**. Place apples, walnuts, raisins,
   flour, ¼ cup of the sugar and 1 teaspoon
   of the cinnamon in **Classic Batter Bowl**;
   mix well. Microwave apple mixture on
   HIGH 3 minutes or until hot; mix well.

2. Separate 12 biscuits. (Discard remaining
   biscuit or set aside for another use.) Using
   lightly floured **Baker's Roller™**, roll each
   biscuit into a 5-inch circle. Combine
   remaining sugar and remaining cinnamon
   in **Small Batter Bowl**. Place ¼ cup of the
   sugar mixture in **Flour/Sugar Shaker**;
   sprinkle evenly over biscuits. Using
   Medium Scoop, divide apple mixture
   evenly onto center of each biscuit.

3. Gather up edges over filling, pinching
   lightly to seal. Place butter in **Small
   Micro-Cooker®**; microwave on HIGH
   20 seconds or until melted. Holding filled
   biscuits at the sealed end, dip each biscuit
   into butter, then into remaining
   cinnamon-sugar mixture in batter bowl.

4. Place biscuits, seam side down, into
   Stoneware Muffin Pan. Cut an "X"
   pattern through the top of each biscuit.
   Bake 25-30 minutes or until golden
   brown. Remove from pan. Serve with ice
   cream, if desired.

Yield: 12 servings

Nutrients per serving: Calories 330, Total Fat 13 g,
Saturated Fat 3 g, Cholesterol less than 5 mg,
Carbohydrate 50 g, Protein 5 g, Sodium 590 mg, Fiber 2 g

Diabetic exchanges per serving: 2 starch, 1 fruit, 2 fat
(3 carb)

Using Medium Scoop,
divide apple mixture
evenly onto center of
each biscuit.

Gather up edges over
filling, pinching lightly
to seal.

Using **Serrated Bread
Knife**, cut an "X" pattern
through the top of each
biscuit.

EASY PEANUT BUTTER PRESSES

Prep time: 10 minutes • Bake time: 12-14 minutes per batch • Cool time: 20 minutes

Just a few ingredients are all you will need to make these flourless peanut butter cookies.

- The **Measure-All®
  Cup** is ideal for
  measuring sticky
  ingredients like
  peanut butter, honey
  and molasses. Its
  unique design allows
  you to push the
  ingredients from the
  cup with little
  cleanup.

- To easily drizzle
  melted chocolate
  over cookies, place
  a small, resealable
  plastic food storage
  bag inside the
  Measure-All Cup.
  Pour melted
  chocolate into corner
  of bag. Twist top of
  bag; secure with a
  Twixit! Clip. Cut a
  small tip off corner
  of bag to allow
  chocolate to flow
  through.

- Small amounts of
  food such as nuts
  can be quickly
  chopped in the
  cap of the **Food
  Chopper**. When
  you are finished
  chopping, simply
  rotate the clear
  plastic collar to
  release it from
  the chopper.

1 cup sugar
1 egg
1 cup creamy peanut butter
½ cup semi-sweet chocolate morsels, melted
2 tablespoons peanuts, chopped

1. Preheat oven to 350°F. In **Classic Batter Bowl**, combine sugar and egg. Add peanut butter; mix until blended.

2. Fit **Cookie Press** with desired disk, making sure the number on the disk is facing outward, away from the dough. Fill Cookie Press with dough. Press dough onto **Rectangle Stone**, 1 inch apart.

3. Bake 12-14 minutes or until cookies are set and light golden brown. Remove from oven; cool 2 minutes on baking stone. Remove to **Stackable Cooling Rack**; cool completely. Repeat with remaining dough.

4. Place chocolate morsels in **Small Micro-Cooker®**; microwave, uncovered, on HIGH 1 minute or until chocolate is melted and smooth, stirring after each 20-second interval. Drizzle chocolate over cookies; sprinkle with peanuts. Let stand until chocolate is set.

Yield: 3 dozen cookies

Nutrients per serving (1 cookie): Calories 80, Total Fat 5 g, Saturated Fat 1 g, Cholesterol 5 mg, Carbohydrate 9 g, Protein 2 g, Sodium 40 mg, Fiber less than 1 g

Diabetic exchanges per serving: ½ starch, 1 fat (½ carb)

APPLE CHERRY TART

Prep time: 30 minutes • Bake time: 30-35 minutes • Cool time: 15 minutes

Looking for a different way to use your round baking stone? Tender apples, tart cherries and a crunchy pecan topping top a pie crust for an extraordinary, easy dessert.

½ package (15 ounces) refrigerated pie crust (1 crust)

⅔ cup all-purpose flour

½ cup packed brown sugar

½ teaspoon **Pantry Korintje Cinnamon**

⅓ cup butter or margarine

½ cup pecan halves, chopped

2 large Granny Smith apples

1 can (21 ounces) cherry pie filling, divided

Thawed, frozen whipped topping or ice cream (optional)

1. Preheat oven to 400°F. Let pie crust stand at room temperature 15 minutes. In **Classic Batter Bowl**, combine flour, brown sugar and cinnamon. Add butter; blend thoroughly using **Pastry Blender**. Chop pecans using **Food Chopper**. Add to batter bowl; mix well and set aside.

2. Roll pie crust into a 13-inch circle on **Classic Round Stone** using lightly floured **Baker's Roller.**™ Peel, core and slice apples using **Apple Peeler/Corer/Slicer**. Cut slices in half; layer apples evenly over crust to within 1 inch of edge of crust.

3. Spread ½ cup of the pie filling over apples; sprinkle flour mixture over apples. Fold outer edge of pastry up over filling to form a 1-inch rim.

4. Bake 30-35 minutes or until crust is golden brown. Remove from oven; cool slightly. Serve warm with remaining pie filling. Top each serving with whipped topping or ice cream, if desired.

Yield: 12 servings

Nutrients per serving: Calories 290, Total Fat 13 g, Saturated Fat 5 g, Cholesterol 15 mg, Carbohydrate 43 g, Protein 2 g, Sodium 130 mg, Fiber 2 g

Diabetic exchanges per serving: 1 starch, 1½ fruit, 2½ fat (3½ carb)

COOK'S TIPS

- Ground cinnamon can be substituted for the Korintje Cinnamon, if desired.

- To heat remaining pie filling, spoon pie filling into **Small Micro-Cooker®**. Microwave, covered, on HIGH 1-2 minutes or until warm.

- Brown sugar is actually granulated sugar with molasses added. The very dark brown sugar tends to have a more pronounced molasses flavor than the lighter varieties. Store brown sugar in a resealable plastic food storage bag in a cool, dry place.

FESTIVE WINTER CRUNCH BARK

Prep time: 25 minutes • Chill time: 30-40 minutes

This simple candy is a perfect holiday treat. Wrap in clear cellophane and add a ribbon or a bow for a great homemade gift.

- Two packages (12 ounces each) premium white or chocolate confectionery coating candy wafers can be substituted for the almond bark, if desired.

- When melting almond bark, make sure the Double Boiler and all utensils are completely dry; even one drop of water will cause almond bark to harden and clump.

- Almond bark can be melted in the microwave oven. Use the **Large Micro-Cooker®** and follow package directions on almond bark for melting in the microwave.

1 package (20 ounces) vanilla- or chocolate-flavored almond bark, coarsely chopped

¾ cup macadamia nuts, coarsely chopped

½ cup sweetened flaked coconut

2 cups crisp rice cereal

1. Preheat oven to 350°F. Line **Stoneware Bar Pan** with a 16-inch piece of **Parchment Paper**, allowing about 6 inches to extend over long sides of pan. In **Professional (2-qt.) Saucepan**, bring 1 inch of water to a simmer over medium-low heat. Coarsely chop almond bark; place in **Double Boiler**. Set Double Boiler over simmering water in saucepan. Melt bark 12-15 minutes or just until melted, stirring occasionally.

2. Meanwhile, coarsely chop nuts with **Food Chopper**. Combine nuts and coconut in **Deep Dish Baker**. Bake 10-12 minutes or until golden brown, stirring occasionally.

3. Stir half of the nut mixture and all of the cereal into melted bark. Remove Double Boiler from saucepan and wipe bottom dry. Pour bark mixture into pan, spreading evenly. Immediately sprinkle with remaining nut mixture; press into bark mixture.

4. Refrigerate 30-40 minutes or until set. Bring edges of Parchment Paper up over bark and break into 2-inch pieces.

Yield: 32 servings

Nutrients per serving: Calories 130, Total Fat 9 g, Saturated Fat .5 g, Cholesterol 0 mg, Carbohydrate 14 g, Protein less than 1 g, Sodium 30 mg, Fiber 0 g

Diabetic exchanges per serving: 1 starch, 1½ fat (1 carb)

Variation: *Festive Cranberry Crunch Bark:* Omit coconut. Substitute almonds, walnuts or pecans for the macadamia nuts. Mix with ¾ cup sweetened dried cranberries. Proceed as recipe directs.

HEAVENLY LEMON ANGEL CAKE

Prep time: 20 minutes • Bake time: 35-40 minutes
Cool time: 1 hour • Stand time: 30 minutes

Tender angel food cake, spiked with a lemony glaze and topped with lightly sweetened raspberries, will have guests asking for seconds.

1 package (16 ounces) angel food cake mix

1-2 lemons

2 cups powdered sugar

2 cups thawed, fat-free frozen whipped topping

1 package (10 ounces) frozen raspberries in syrup, thawed

1. Preheat oven to 350°F. Prepare cake mix according to package directions. Pour batter into ungreased **Rectangular Baker**, spreading evenly. Bake on center rack in oven 35-40 minutes or until top of cake is golden brown, cracked and firm to the touch. Do not underbake. Remove from oven. Using **Oven Mitts**, carefully invert baker onto **Stackable Cooling Rack**; cool completely. (Do not remove cake from baker.)

2. Turn baker upright; poke holes in cake about 1½ inches deep and ½ inch apart with large fork. Zest one lemon using **Lemon Zester/Scorer** to measure 1 tablespoon zest. Juice lemons using **Juicer** to measure ¼ cup juice.

3. In **Small Batter Bowl**, combine powdered sugar, lemon juice and zest; whisk until smooth. Slowly pour glaze over cake, spreading evenly. Let stand 30 minutes or until glaze is set.

4. Attach open star tip to **Easy Accent®
Decorator**; fill with whipped topping. Cut cake into squares. Garnish each serving with whipped topping; top with raspberries.

Yield: 15 servings

Low Fat Nutrients per serving: Calories 200, Total Fat 0 g, Saturated Fat 0 g, Cholesterol 0 mg, Carbohydrate 46 g, Protein 3 g, Sodium 270 mg, Fiber 1 g

Diabetic exchanges per serving: 1 starch, 2 fruit (3 carb)

COOK'S TIPS

■ Fresh raspberries, tossed with 1-2 tablespoons granulated sugar, can be substituted for the frozen raspberries, if desired.

■ You can prepare this cake ahead of time through Step 1. When the cake is completely cooled, tent the baker loosely with aluminum foil until you are ready to serve the cake; proceed as recipe directs.

■ To cut easily through angel food cake, use a gentle sawing motion with the **Serrated Bread Knife**.

TIRAMISU BROWNIE SQUARES

Prep time: 20 minutes • Cool time: 1 hour
Bake time: 25-30 minutes • Chill time: 30 minutes

These layered brownie bars are topped with a creamy, coffee-flavored filling that is studded with chunks of chocolate cookies. What a treat!

■ Ground cinnamon can be substituted for the Korintje Cinnamon, if desired.

■ To easily cut this dessert into squares, use the **Utility Knife** that has been dipped in hot water. Serve using the **Mini-Serving Spatula**.

■ Save time by preparing the brownie squares several hours in advance. You'll want to keep the dessert refrigerated until it is ready to serve.

1 package (19-21 ounces) brownie mix (plus ingredients to make cake-like brownies)
1 cup milk
¼ cup instant coffee granules
1 container (12 ounces) frozen whipped topping, thawed, divided
2 packages (3.4 ounces each) cheesecake instant pudding and pie filling
20 chocolate creme-filled sandwich cookies, coarsely chopped (2 cups)
2 tablespoons semi-sweet chocolate morsels, grated
¼ teaspoon **Pantry Korintje Cinnamon**

1. Preheat oven to 350°F. Lightly spray **Rectangular Baker** with nonstick cooking spray. Prepare brownie mix according to package directions for cake-like brownies; pour batter into baker, spreading evenly. Bake 25-30 minutes or until **Cake Tester** inserted in center comes out clean. Remove from oven; cool completely.

2. In **Classic Batter Bowl**, combine milk and instant coffee granules; stir until dissolved. Add half of the whipped topping and all of the pudding mix; whisk until smooth. Coarsely chop cookies using **Food Chopper**; fold into pudding mixture. Spread filling evenly over brownie.

3. Attach open star tip to **Easy Accent®** **Decorator**; fill with remaining whipped topping. Pipe whipped topping in diagonal rows, ¼ inch apart, over filling. Grate chocolate morsels over whipped topping using **Deluxe Cheese Grater**. Sprinkle with cinnamon using **Flour/Sugar Shaker**. Refrigerate at least 30 minutes. Cut into squares.

Yield: 20 servings

Nutrients per serving: Calories 330, Total Fat 16 g, Saturated Fat 4.5 g, Cholesterol 35 mg, Carbohydrate 43 g, Protein 3 g, Sodium 310 mg, Fiber 0 g

Diabetic exchanges per serving: 1 starch, 2 fruit, 3 fat (3 carb)

QUICK PUMPKIN SPICE CAKE

Prep time: 15 minutes • Microwave time: 14 minutes
Stand time: 10 minutes • Cool time: 30 minutes

A comforting, spicy aroma will fill the air when you make this simple cake.
The pumpkin adds moisture naturally, so no oil is needed for this recipe.

Cake

- 3 eggs, lightly beaten
- 1 can (15 ounces) solid pack pumpkin
- 1 package (18.25 ounces) spice cake mix

Glaze

- 1 cup powdered sugar
- 3-4 teaspoons milk
- 1 orange
- 12 pecan halves (optional)

1. For cake, brush **Stoneware Fluted Pan** with vegetable oil using **Pastry Brush**. In **Classic Batter Bowl**, combine eggs and pumpkin; whisk until smooth. Add cake mix; whisk until thoroughly blended, about 1 minute. Pour batter into pan, spreading evenly.

2. Microwave cake on HIGH 14 minutes or until **Cake Tester** inserted near center comes out clean. (Cake will be slightly moist on top near center.) Let stand in microwave 10 minutes. If necessary, loosen cake from sides of pan; invert onto serving plate. Cool at least 30 minutes.

3. For glaze, in **Small Batter Bowl**, combine powdered sugar and 3-4 teaspoons milk to make a thick glaze. Zest orange using **Lemon Zester/Scorer**. Spread glaze over top of cake. Arrange pecan halves evenly over top of cake, if desired; sprinkle with orange zest. Let stand until glaze is set before slicing.

Yield: 12 servings

Nutrients per serving: Calories 250, Total Fat 7 g, Saturated Fat 2 g, Cholesterol 65 mg, Carbohydrate 45 g, Protein 5 g, Sodium 350 mg, Fiber 2 g

Diabetic exchanges per serving: 2 starch, 1 fruit, 1 fat (3 carb)

Variation: *Quick Chocolate Cherry Cake:* Substitute 1 can (21 ounces) cherry pie filling for the pumpkin and 1 package (18.25 ounces) chocolate cake mix for the spice cake mix. Add pie filling and cake mix to eggs; whisk until thoroughly blended, about 1 minute. Proceed as recipe directs. Omit orange zest and pecans.

Nutrients per serving: Calories 260, Total Fat 8 g, Saturated Fat 2 g, Cholesterol 55 mg, Carbohydrate 46 g, Protein 4 g, Sodium 380 mg, Fiber 1 g

Diabetic exchanges per serving: 1 starch, 2 fruit, 1½ fat (3 carb)

FRUIT-TOPPED TRIPLE CHOCOLATE PIZZA

Prep time: 30 minutes • Bake time: 12-15 minutes
Cool time: 1 hour • Chill time: 30 minutes

Refrigerated chocolate chip cookie dough makes a convenient crust for this dessert pizza featuring a white chocolate filling and a colorful fruit topping.

- It's important to use a Large Round Stone for this recipe as the cookie dough crust spreads during baking.

- Strawberries can become waterlogged if exposed to water for too long. Gently wash strawberries and pat dry just before using them.

1 package (18 ounces) refrigerated chocolate chip cookie dough
2 squares (1 ounce each) white chocolate for baking
2 tablespoons milk
1 package (8 ounces) cream cheese, softened
¼ cup powdered sugar
1 cup thawed, frozen whipped topping
12-16 strawberries, cut in half
1 can (11 ounces) mandarin orange segments, well drained
¼ cup semi-sweet chocolate morsels
1 teaspoon vegetable oil

1. Preheat oven to 350°F. Shape cookie dough into a ball and place in center of **Large Round Stone**. Using lightly floured **Baker's Roller**™, roll dough to a 12-inch circle, about ¼ inch thick. Bake 12-15 minutes or until edges are set. (Cookie will be soft. Do not overbake.) Remove from oven; cool 10 minutes. Carefully loosen cookie from baking stone using **Serrated Bread Knife**; cool completely on baking stone.

2. Place white chocolate and milk in **Small Batter Bowl**. Microwave on HIGH 1 minute; stir until chocolate is melted and mixture is smooth. Microwave an additional 10-20 seconds if necessary. Cool slightly. In **Classic Batter Bowl**, combine cream cheese and powdered sugar; mix well. Gradually stir in white chocolate mixture; mix until smooth. Fold in whipped topping. Spread cream cheese mixture evenly over cookie.

3. Arrange strawberries and mandarin oranges over cream cheese mixture. Place chocolate morsels and vegetable oil in **Small Micro-Cooker®**; microwave, uncovered, on HIGH 30 seconds or until chocolate is melted and smooth. Drizzle over fruit. Refrigerate at least 30 minutes. Cut into wedges.

Yield: 16 servings

Nutrients per serving: Calories 260, Total Fat 15 g, Saturated Fat 8 g, Cholesterol 20 mg, Carbohydrate 29 g, Protein 3 g, Sodium 150 mg, Fiber 1 g

Diabetic exchanges per serving: 1 starch, 1 fruit, 3 fat (2 carb)

INDEX

About Our Recipes

All recipes were developed and tested in The Pampered Chef® Test Kitchens by professional home economists. For best results, we recommend you use the ingredients indicated in the recipe. The preparation and cooking times at the beginning of each recipe serve as a helpful guide when planning your time in the kitchen. As an important first step, we suggest you read through the recipe and assemble the necessary ingredients and equipment. "Prep time" is the approximate amount of time needed to prepare recipe ingredients before a final "Cook time." Prep time includes active steps such as chopping and mixing. It can also include cooking ingredients for a recipe that is assembled and then baked. Some preparation steps can be done simultaneously or during cooking and are usually indicated by the term "meanwhile." Some recipes that have steps not easily separated have a combined "Prep and cook time."

Notes on Nutrition

The nutrition information in *All The Best* can help you decide how specific recipes can fit into your overall meal plan. At the end of each recipe, we list calories, total fat, saturated fat, cholesterol, carbohydrate, protein, sodium and fiber. We also include diabetic exchange information commonly used by people with diabetes. This information is based on the 1995 *Exchange Lists for Meal Planning* by the American Diabetes Association and the American Dietetic Association. For each recipe, two lists of exchanges are provided. The first option is based on the traditional method of figuring diabetic exchanges; the second option is given in parentheses and reflects the newer system of carbohydrate counting. If you use the exchanges, consult your doctor, certified diabetes educator or registered dietitian.

Nutritional analysis for each recipe is based on the first ingredient listed whenever a choice is given and does not include optional ingredients, garnishes, fat used to grease pans, or serving suggestions. The ingredients used in our recipes and for nutritional analyses are based on most commonly purchased foods and unless indicated otherwise use 2 percent reduced-fat milk and large eggs. Recipes requiring ground beef are analyzed based on 90 percent lean ground beef. Recipes requiring ground turkey are analyzed based on 93 percent lean ground turkey. When margarine is an ingredient option, use a product containing 80 percent fat and not vegetable oil spread. Recipes labeled as *Low Fat* have 3 grams or less fat per serving.

Metric Conversion Chart

Volume Measurements (dry)	Volume Measurements (fluid)	Dimensions
⅛ teaspoon = 0.6 mL	1 fluid ounce (2 tablespoons) = 30 mL	⅛ inch = 3 mm
¼ teaspoon = 1.25 mL	4 fluid ounces (½ cup) = 125 mL	¼ inch = 6 mm
½ teaspoon = 2.5 mL	8 fluid ounces (1 cup) = 250 mL	½ inch = 1 cm
¾ teaspoon = 3.75 mL	12 fluid ounces (1½ cups) = 375 mL	¾ inch = 2 cm
1 teaspoon = 5 mL	16 fluid ounces (2 cups) = 500 mL	1 inch = 2.5 cm
1 tablespoon = 15 mL		
2 tablespoons = 30 mL	**Weights (mass)**	**Oven Temperatures**
¼ cup = 50 mL		250°F = 120°C
⅓ cup = 75 mL	1 ounce = 30 g	275°F = 140°C
½ cup = 125 mL	4 ounces = 125 g	300°F = 150°C
⅔ cup = 150 mL	8 ounces = 250 g	325°F = 160°C
¾ cup = 175 mL	12 ounces = 350 g	350°F = 180°C
1 cup = 250 mL	16 ounces = 1 pound = 500 g	375°F = 190°C
		400°F = 200°C
		425°F = 220°C
		450°F = 230°C

Recipes in this cookbook have not been tested using metric measures. When converting and preparing recipes with metric measures, some variations in quality may be noticed.